THIS SIDE OF A
 - Daniel J. Rice

THE UNPEOPLED SEASON: Journal from a North Country Wilderness (2014)
 - Daniel J. Rice

WITHIN THESE WOODS: A collection of Northwoods nature essays with original illustrations by the author (2015)
 - Timothy Goodwin

RELENTLESS: A Striker Mystery Novel (2015)
 - Marcus Bruning & Jen Wright

ECOLOGICAL IDENTITY: Finding your place in a biological world (2016)
 - Timothy Goodwin

TEACHERS IN THE FOREST: Essays from the last wilderness in Mississippi Headwaters country (2016)
 - Barry Babcock

YOUNG BUT FREE: A Novel (coming 2017)
 - Daniel J. Rice

MANY THINGS: A series of 5 children's books about the senses, in English and Ojibwe language (coming 2017)
 -Erika Bailey-Johnson

RIVERFEET PRESS ANTHOLOGY (coming 2017)
 - Various authors of poetry, fiction & non-fiction

available wherever books are sold, or on our webpage:
www.riverfeetpress.com

"*Practice Non-interference, I will walk with you. Everything we do is within a circle. If we miss it, keep walking. We don't go back. It will come around again. We keep walking the circle and pick it up on the next round. Just keep walking.*" ~Larry Stillday (Gichi-Ma'iingan/Big Wolf) Obaashiing.

Dedication:

This book is dedicated to my wife Barbara Ann, our daughters Kimberly Irene and Erin Marie, our grandchildren Travis Michael and Kelly Jean, and to all those who walked with or have been touched by the words and teachings of Larry Stillday.

Riverfeet Press
Bemidji, MN
Livingston, MT
www.riverfeetpress.com

ROAD TO PONEMAH
The Teachings of Larry Stillday
Michael Meuers
Non-Fiction

Cover design by Daniel J. Rice
Cover photo by the author
Author photo by Image Photography, Bemidji

Table of Contents:

ROAD TO PONEMAH

The Teachings of Larry Stillday

by Michael Meuers

Author's Note

It is my view that we need to recognize and learn more about how Indian culture, politics, gender roles, spirituality, and the important yet largely unrecognized role it has played in this country's identity. This indigenous culture still lives…although hidden to those not looking. In my view, it would benefit the citizens of the US and Canada to do a bit of "assimilating" with Turtle Island's (America's) First Peoples, in order to learn more of what they have to teach us…and themselves…about the spirit of this land and its' Sacred places. After all, primally, we are ALL tribal people. It's just that European Americans are further away from our tribal roots in time and space than are our Indigenous brothers and sisters.

Preface

When the Time is Right, Write.

Boozhoo: An Irishman in Ojibwe Country

Humor permeates the culture. It is often self-deprecating and rarely caustic. The sense of humor I hear and see in Indian Country always delights.

Being a mixed blood American without tradition in the sense of my ancestors, I am neither German, nor French, nor Irish culturally. Perhaps because Irish blood flows through my veins in twice the amount of German or French, I relate more to the Irish. Or perhaps it is because I have been blessed with a touch of the blarney.

During the mid-60's I lived in Hawaii and Korea courtesy of the United States Army. I was intrigued by how different things were from the life I had growing up in a Twin Cities suburb. I found interest in and enjoyed learning about the history, culture, and language of these peoples.

In my mid-30's I moved to Bemidji, MN to finish my last two years of college. Since a child, I'd always loved "going up north."

Before moving to Minnesota's Great North Woods, I knew little of American Indians. Soon I heard of "Indian Time." At first I thought it to be a light-hearted disparagement used by Indian and non-Indian alike to denote tardiness. I later learned it to be a multi-layered concept of time practiced by America's Indigenous people. I realized I was in the midst of a different culture without leaving home.

I grew up with a great compassion and admiration for historical Indians,

though contemporary Indian culture was unknown to me. An interest in politics brought me into contact with Indian leaders, and in 1994, I was hired by the Red Lake Band of Chippewa Indians for my experience in political and public relations.

I've worked with the Red Lake Ojibwe now for over two decades. I was hired by the Tribal Council to go out and find good news, then write stories and take photos of it in order to balance what often seemed a media concentration on bad news coming from the reservation. During this fruitful time, I learned of a different heritage whose people laugh easily, hold sacred the land, and respect their elders, the Indigenous culture of these woodlands.

Bemidji is surrounded by Minnesota's three largest reservations: the Red Lake, Leech Lake, and White Earth Indian Nations. Non-Indians have lived in the Bemidji area for little more than a century. By working with American Indians, I have learned that the greater history, culture, and spirit of these woodlands, is Ojibwe. I came to this place to study mass communications at a State University, but graduated to learn of an ancient land and it's heritage.

Reflections on the Gichi-Ziibi (Big River/Mississippi)

Perhaps had we not conquered but assimilated with this land it would have truly been a new world…which would have been the courteous and respectful thing to do.

I learned "out the gate" enough about Ojibwe culture to understand that they have a great respect for the environment and for elders. It's part of their world-view. This alone is enough to make me wonder if we'd have a better American culture by adopting these values from our aboriginal neighbors – the culture of the land. I often wonder if we would have a better America if we had assimilated with the Indigenous populations of Turtle Island, rather than destroying the culture, stealing the continent, and replanting a culture we claimed to have wanted to escape.

If land is related to nature and nature to God, then this land is sacred. Nearly all of us are the sons and daughters of immigrants. It's my view that if we claim this land, then we claim its' history as well. I find it arrogant of us to pretend that history began upon our arrival in Bemidji in 1895, or Minnesota in 1858, or 1776 or 1640 or 1492. What other immigrants of the world count the beginning of its history with their arrival?

Furthermore, I submit we should also give great respect, even celebrate the Indigenous Culture of the land. To learn of this Indigenous knowledge, who better to teach about this land we claim than the long-time stewards of this land whose ancestors are buried beneath our feet?

It is not difficult for me to dream of a time when we will adopt, and/or adapt, many American Indigenous values, the greatest of which is a respect for all living things and recognizing our true role in the Circle of Life. The alternative is to not make a change, and continue on our current path of destruction.

Even beautifully decorated lies are never as impressive as simple truths.

How much more do we think Mother Earth will tolerate? Our Earth Mother is getting irked. Everything is out of balance, but She WILL heal her wounds just as every other living thing does. Do we doubt that?

Perhaps our Indigenous friends will remind us (and themselves) of our collective tribal roots, and teach us about the land on which we live. Those who approach the land with respect and a true heart will learn of these secrets. When one is fortunate enough to be exposed to exceptional teachers, learning comes more quickly.

Larry Stillday was one such teacher. He would say, "People and culture change but the teachings do not. Approach such matters with the Medicine of the Wolf, and that is humility."

Larry seemed inspired, or at least attentive to how he formed his arguments and with the words he chose. His gift was to be able to touch the primal, to remind us of things we already knew, and to help facilitate that "aha" moment.

Universality was something Larry always emphasized. In the coming readings, you'll unlikely find anything new, or anything you haven't heard or read or thought about before. Larry would say the reason for this is because the Creator gave everyone the same instructions. Larry's words are just said in a different way, in a language that lives in the land on which we live. They may be different words, but are the same concepts; the same symbols, but taught by a First American, a humble, gentle and wise man who lived just up the road.

"I always learn something from listening, especially from listening to people that have wisdom inside, and seem to be unaware that it is something special to many others that stand not where they stand." ~Frank Meuers

Introduction:

Gichi-Ma'iingan, Gaa-izhinikaanid

(Big Wolf, The One who named me)

I don't remember how I met Larry Stillday. How could I know at the time that this might be important?

Lawrence Edward Stillday, Sr., whose Spirit or Indian name was Gichi-Ma'iingan (Big Wolf), was a fluent Ojibwemowin (Ojibwe language) First Speaker with extensive knowledge on traditional, medicine wheel, and sweat lodge teachings. He was a Spiritual/Cultural Advisor for many tribal programs.

Many were attracted to his manner of teaching about the Gifts of the Seven Grandfathers, and using the Medicine Wheel as a symbol and teaching tool for Wellness, Balance and understanding the Circle of Life.

Ultimately, he was recognized as a teacher, but also a healer, and a spiritual leader. Larry, however, would never describe himself by any of these titles. He would leave those labels or descriptions to others. To do otherwise might be seen as presumptuous, less than humble, and humility was among his virtues.

In Ojibwe tradition, true leadership requires humility. One does not apply for leadership. Leadership then is left for others to determine. Larry would have said that leadership is a one of responsibility, not of power.

******

Gichi-Ma'iingan (Larry) was born on May 14, 1944, six months and ten days my elder. He grew up in Ponemah, the heart of the Red Lake Nation where Ojibwe culture and language survive. He was a member of the Makwa Doodem (Bear Clan), of the Red Lake Band of Chippewa Indians.

Larry was a Vietnam Veteran and a member of the Ponemah Three Star Warrior Society. After four years of service in the US Army, he was discharged and moved to the Twin Cities area.

In 1999 he moved back home to Ponemah with his future wife, a Louisiana Belle named Violet. As a well-respected spiritual advisor, his passion was helping people with the journey of their lives. He walked with many and participated in numerous projects both on and off Red Lake Nation.

He was both nephew and student of Tommy J. Stillday. Tom, also a Spiritual Leader, was well known, colorful, and highly respected by many.

Gichi-Ma'iingan was the inspiration behind the Red Lake Coalition, a reservation-wide community organization that helped coordinate Healing Day and other wellness type events. Larry and Violet hosted what was billed as a Healing Sweat Lodge, from time to time, in the backwoods of Ponemah. The Lodge welcomed all nations. All were welcome that approached learning with a true heart.

Gichi-Ma'iingan was heavily involved in the language and cultural revitalization efforts at Red Lake, and served as its spiritual/cultural advisor. He was the spiritual advisor for many tribal programs on the reservation including the Red Lake DNR, Equay [Ikwewag] Wiigamig, (Women's Shelter) Red Lake Nation College, and Chemical Health programs, just to name a few.

Employed by Red Lake Chemical Health programs for 14 years, in late 2013 he retired as supervisor of the Ponemah Outpatient Chemical Health Program.

During that retirement, Larry was a sought after teacher recognized for his traditional teachings. He conducted sensitivity trainings around the state including the Mayo Clinic, the Minnesota Department of Human Services, and multiple Christian churches. He was visited regularly by young people with a desire to learn of Ojibwe culture, which included the Archdiocese of St. Paul Mission to Red Lake, students of Cretin-Derham Hall High School in St. Paul, and Penn State students, among others.

Less than a year after retiring and six days after his 70th birthday, Larry died in his sleep on the morning of Tuesday, May 20, 2014. Larry lived with his wife Violet in Kelliher, MN, an off-reservation community just east of Ponemah. Violet was a great help to Larry in his work and was seen most often at his side.

A Visit with Violet

On July 28, 2014 at 3 pm at the Country Kitchen in Bemidji, I visited with Larry's widow Violet Stillday.

I had thought for some time that Larry had a very special gift, he was inspired and inspiring. I often wondered, and still do, about his gift for teaching this simple yet profound way of living. One who has walked with Larry knows of what I speak. I asked Violet about his gift.

"He had a vision that he was to speak for his people."

"This was a dream. I was looking down from the sky, and the lakes were lungs. I am going to be the door to the lodge. I have checked on the lodge and can see much abuse going on." ~Gichi-Ma'iingan

Larry met Violet in Louisiana in 1998. He was later living in Willmar, MN and she joined him. They'd come up to Ponemah and stayed with Bonnie Rose Cloud, (Larry's sister) and moved up permanently in 1999.

In 2000 Tommy J. married Larry and Violet but had a Leech Lake woman, Helen Condo, come over and assist him. They married behind the powwow grounds in Ponemah on the lake. "We had a trellis. It was very nice," she said.

But when Larry and Violet took the marriage certificate to be filed, the auditor said it wasn't legal as Tommy J was not a preacher. When Tommy learned of this, he got irked, and drove down to the auditor's office with his Minnesota Secretary of State "Blue Book" on elections. He showed her the 1996 edition identifying Tom, (including his photo and bio) as being the Chaplin of the Minnesota State Senate for two years." (Tom was the first non-Judeo/Christian ever to serve in that capacity) They honored the marriage.

On August 31, 1999 when the couple came back to Ponemah, Larry and Violet began preparing for the Healing Sweat Lodge (The future Obaashiing University). "It was small at first, just doing sweats," said Violet. "The Penn State kids helped prepare for the Wellness Day, it got bigger and bigger."

They held a *Wellbriety* event for a few years, but it was a lot of work and they weren't getting much help. They decided if no one helped they'd drop it and would do the Wellness Day at what was to become Obaashiing University.

"In 2007 Tommy J. was getting sick," said Violet. "Tom was, among other things, the spiritual advisor for powwows. Sickly, he recommended Larry take his place, and Larry did. In October 2008 Tommy J. died. Powwow organizers kept asking Larry to do invocations for powwows." His vision was coming true.

Then on May 25, 2010 they hosted the first Wellness Lodge. (I attended them all, this one and the remaining four.) In 2010 there were two, one also in the fall. The Lodge was then held annually in late summer of 2011, 2012, and 2013. The sixth lodge was scheduled for June 10, 2014, but never to be.

She didn't know why he died. Diabetes messes with the heart a bit, she said. There was lots of madness with the EMT's trying to resuscitate Larry when she knew he was dead. A woman cop stayed with her the entire time. Rose and Vickie (Larry's sister and niece) came over, and then a lot of family and friends began appearing.

Violet was changing a light bulb a short time after Larry's death. She said she got pissed at Larry, as she hadn't had to do that in 15 years. She thinks 200 people could have been at the June 10, 2014 Lodge – had it occurred - because all the Penn State folks were coming. All the first-language people would have been there, and more. I agreed, and told her I had mentioned to Larry that there could be a crowd, and asked if he was he ready for it.

Violet and I chatted about what that would have been like, if Larry had gotten that kind of following, when they were busier than heck as it was.

Before our visit ended, Violet told me she witnessed Larry's Midewiwin 1st Degree ceremony. (According to historian Michael Angel, the Midewiwin is a "flexible, tenacious tradition that provided an institutional setting for the teaching of the world view – or religious beliefs - of the Ojibwa people.")

At another ceremony she said she waited in the car while all the others were inside the ceremonial lodge. She read until dark, and then just sat enjoying a nice evening. When participants came out to gather around the fire, Violet decided she would join them.

Arriving at the fire Tommy J. asked Violet where she had been. "You should have been here," Tom said, "because Misaabe (Bigfoot or Wilderness man) could have gotten you." Who knows if or how serious he was. He often teased, but maybe not. Misaabe is a benevolent creature of traditional Ojibwe culture and represents Honesty in the Teachings of the Seven Grandfathers.

Before Violet left, we talked of my possible plans to document Larry's teachings because I had written and witnessed so much. She said simply, "I think it's supposed to happen, I like your thinking on it."

*****

Five months later, I wrote Violet to tell her that I had started the book by gathering all my notes, stories, and the PowerPoint teachings into several files and sub-files. "It's strange," I wrote, "I feel this great compassion for you as I'm engaged in the gathering of his words. I'm missing him deeply, so I can't imagine what it must be like for you."

"By the way, the number of people Larry touched amazes me," I continued. "Every time I put up a quote with a photo of Larry on Facebook, I get much positive feedback. It is one of many motives that make me write. Knowing that I'll be able to share his words with all those folks sometime soon pleases me."

I went on to tell her, "When you and Larry would present a teaching, the one big problem always was; if something heavy was said, a mind wanders reflecting on that. But the teaching goes on, and who knows what we've missed, yet we have. This book will allow all those folks to reflect as long as they want on some such illumination and know they will not miss a thing being able to return to the page at will.

"I learn new things each time I read my collection of words, so by writing about Larry he continues to teach me. For this I am grateful. I have been told that Larry watches over this project. That is encouraging. I do not doubt it."

Violet responded later. "I am so happy you have undertaken this huge project. I know Larry would want you to do it. Thank you for thinking of me. As I've said before, I do hope to be of some help to you. Please let me know what I can do."

A Gathering of Clans

"It was explained that in past times when there were troubles within tribes, the heads of the clans gathered to discuss resolutions of the problem." ~Gichi-Ma'iingan

Larry Stillday (Gichi-Ma'iingan/Big Wolf) of Obaashiing (Ponemah) was a respected teacher, healer and spiritual and cultural advisor. To me, he just seemed to "appear" a few years ago.

The first time I remember seeing the name Larry Stillday was in December 2008 after the death of Larry's mentor Thomas J, that October. He was beginning a more visible public life, taking on many of the spiritual advisor duties of Tommy J., although I did not know this at the time, nor did I meet Larry until later.

One day I saw Larry's and Violet's names in an invitation to a "Gathering of the Clans & Potluck Feast at Ponemah Center." The wording on the invitation caught my eye as something a bit different, something with a greater breadth than events I was used to. It was mixing culture with problem solving. It was worded thus:

"It was explained that in past times when there were troubles within tribes, the heads of the clans gathered to discuss resolutions of the problem. With this in mind and knowing that we each belong to a clan, Red Lake White Bison Coalition and Red Lake Project Safe Neighborhoods will begin hosting a Seasonal Gathering of the Clans in our communities. These quarterly gatherings will be held in each village on a rotating basis and will cover issues that concern our people.

The first Seasonal Gathering of the Clans will be held on Monday, December 22nd at 5:30 pm in the village of O-Bah-Shing. (Obaashiing) *Our first topic will be 'Violence touches us all.' Please join us for an evening to listen to presentations, and participate in discussion about how violence touches each and every one of us in some form.*

Custom teaches us to feed our visitors so a potluck meal will be available for everyone participating. Please invite an elder or young person, offer a ride, bring a dish, or just come by yourself. The only way to overcome troubling issues is to stand up and face them head on. Healing begins with each and every one of us having the courage to step forward, let your voice be heard, let your words be kind and productive, let us walk our talk, and let it begin with me!"

My notes tell me the first time I met, and then mentioned Larry in a press release was the following February (2009) at the Third Annual Drug and Gang Conference. I was still unaware that he was a cultural/spiritual leader and I didn't identify him as such. I did say that there was, "…an opening prayer by Mr. Larry Stillday," but that was not unusual for any elder, particularly a First (Ojibwe) Speaker to give an invocation. (In hindsight, I know that at this time he was the cultural/spiritual advisor for Chemical Health Programs.)

Later in the same story I wrote, "The session was presented by Larry Stillday, Ponemah Out-patient supervisor now for seven years, and Violet Stillday, CD Counselor with Red Lake Chemical Health. Larry Stillday, among many of his activities, is an adjunct professor at Bemidji State University. Violet Stillday has an impressive training resume and is the current chair of 7 Clans *Wellbriety* Coalition."

"Join the Voices of Recovery: Together We Learn, Together We Heal."

It was in September of 2009 when I first visited with Larry and more fully realized he might be a different kind of spiritual leader than which I was familiar. There was to be a gathering billed as a Kick-off to National Alcohol and Drug Addiction Recovery and Native American *Wellbriety* Month. As the Public Relations person for the Red Lake Band, this was an easy story to cover as chemical health has my interest.

Better yet, the event was not held at Red Lake but at Bemidji's downtown lake front near the iconic statues of Paul and Babe, not far from my home. This was unusual, Indian events didn't happen in this border town known as Bemidji (from the Ojibwe word Bemijigamaag) a community near the center of Minnesota's three largest Indian Reservations.

Although I didn't yet seem to realize he was a healer and teacher, this was evidence Larry was reaching out to all colors, not just Indians. Also unusual, the event was supported by the city with a Mayoral Proclamation declaring a *Wellbriety* month in Bemidji. The mayor called upon the people of Bemidji to observe the month with appropriate programs, activities and ceremonies supporting the year's theme, "Join the Voices of Recovery."

My first reference of Larry as a Spiritual Leader came at the Drug and Gang Conference of February 2010 sponsored by the tribe's chemical health programs.

Most, if not all, tribal programs have a Spiritual/Cultural Advisor, something seldom seen in off-reservation communities in my experience. I soon learned that Larry was the advisor for many of the programs I covered as administration priorities as well as my own interest. As I saw more and more of him, I found myself listening closer, and writing down his words. There was something different about him.

His words seemed inspired to me, to have a certain poetic nature about them, or a feeling of universality. Little by little I paid even closer attention to him.

Two months later, on May 25, 2010, I began to realize more fully what an unusual person Larry was when I attended the first all-day Teaching, which Larry hosted in the backwoods near Ponemah at Obaashiing University. He referred to it as a Healing Lodge, or Wellness Day.

Feast and Sacred Fire in Support of the Homeless

By the time December 2010 rolled around, both my wife Barbara and I were friendly with Larry and Violet. Barbara works with the homeless in Bemidji and came along with me for a Christmas Party at the Homeless Shelter in Red Lake celebrating a "Feast and Fire in Support of National Homeless Persons' Memorial Day," an event held annually on or about the first day of winter, which is the most difficult season for homeless people in northern Minnesota.

A Memorial Fire was kindled at dawn and would burn until dusk, with a ceremony and feast to begin at 11 a.m. While waiting to speak, Larry conducted an invocation that included smudging with sage after which he performed a pipe ceremony. Finishing, he spoke to the group. "We must remember that this can happen to anybody. Many of us are only one pay check away from being homeless." Stillday went on to say that he himself was homeless (living on the streets) for two years after returning from Viet Nam. "I am glad the Tribal Council is doing something in this area. This is all part of the healing. We want to thank the Fire, the Drum, and all of you." Stillday then called on the Drum for a song of healing. A spirit dish was prepared, and many offered tobacco at the memorial fire.

Sufficiently impressed with his message, I now made it a point to show up at as many events involving Larry that I could. I was often invited by Larry to come to his more formal teachings.

Prologue:

Ticket to Write

"I want to thank you for being the messenger of the teachings." ~Larry Stillday

As I got to know Larry Stillday better, I found myself writing more about culture and at times, things that might be defined as spiritual. I had learned early that one does not take photos of ceremony. I thought it best then to ask Larry if it was okay to write of his teachings, which certainly were cultural and therefore spiritual; being two parts of the same thing - a way of life.

On Wednesday August 22, 2012 at 4:05 p.m. I wrote to Larry. "Chi Ma'iingan, do you mind if I write about your teachings for the tribal newspaper or my blog? I think you have so much to share that would benefit Indian and non-Indian alike. But I won't if you think I should not. Weweni, (carefully) Makakii*."

(*Makakii a nickname for me favored by Ponemah folk, short for Omakakii meaning frog)

Larry replied: "Hey Makakii, Do you think it's something people would read about? You know if this can help someone along the way, then it should be out there to help whoever may be in need of direction. Chi Ma'iingan."

"Chi Ma'iingan, I do," I answered. "I was hoping you would say such. I will write something for the tribal newspaper, and then I will write something for my blog where I can be a little more mystical. Both Indian and non-Indian have told me that they liked what I wrote about the Seven Fires Prophecy. I will send you a couple of links; including one I wrote about the first healing lodge I attended. I will send those soon. Chi-miigwech, (thanks much) - Makakii"

I proceeded to send Larry links to three stories along with this note, "Chi Ma'iingan, The first story is on the Healing Lodge. I hope I could write it better now that I know more. I would be interested in your feedback on my writings. I feel I may be in an interesting position to share this with Chi-Mookomaanan. (White folks/Americans, literally Big Knives) The second is the story I wrote about the dedication of the Ponemah Round House, and the third is a memorial I wrote on the passing of Tommy J. Again, I would be appreciative if you think I am doing justice to these subjects and if you have any advice for me. Miigwech. - Makakii"

Larry replied, "Those are good articles, it's the first time I saw them. As I read them it opened a lot more and beyond. I want to thank you for being the messenger of the teachings. I'll be looking forward for the next article. When and if people make comments tell them they're welcome to contact Violet or me. Miigwech Makakii"

From Larry at Language Summit Presentation, December 18, 2013

"I'm gonna talk about some teachings, some time-honored teachings. These sacred teachings, ya know they didn't go away. They never went away. They didn't go anywhere. So follow along on this PowerPoint. I'm trying to make it so you can visually see as we go through these.

"When I first got home, I started putting our language and the teachings on a PowerPoint, and I was told I wasn't supposed to do that. But like I've always done in my life, I didn't listen. I went right ahead and did it. So those of you, my elders here, I apologize. I ask them for permission to talk about the teachings. That I, myself, learned. And so we're gonna go through this again, I'd like to have you participate."

******

Note: All of Larry's words, with few exceptions, were heard by me, read by me, or given to me directly from Larry or Violet such as the PowerPoint section. I quote no one else unless identified. I don't rely on memory. My words or those of others are clearly marked.

My goal, from the beginning of this effort, has been to share with the reader ALL of the words and teachings of Larry Stillday that are in my possession.

I use the "double vowel system" of spelling for Ojibwemowin. Larry uses both the "double vowel" system and "folk" spelling. Folk spelling is used by many First Speakers and is spelled the way the speaker hears the word, often using hyphens to form the many compound words. In order to teach and read the language, a consistent form a spelling was needed, of which the "double vowel system" is the most popular among US Ojibwe Nations.

Part 1

Four Years at Obaashiing University

May 2010, Notes from a Healing Lodge #1

"Indians think in a circular rather than in a linear manner. That's why time seems less important, which is better for stress. Take things as they come." ~Gichi-Ma'iin-gan

If I was going anywhere else, I'd be late. It was 8:30 a.m. on a beautiful morning in late May 2010. I was traveling north on Beltrami County Road 15 from Bemidji, Minnesota. Just north of Nebish Township, (a corruption of the word Aniibiish in Ojibwe meaning leaf or tea) I noticed a sudden change in landscape. I had gone from farmland to forest. I was on the Red Lake Indi-

an Reservation. I was no longer on Beltrami County 15, but on Reservation Highway 18. I was heading deep into Ojibwe Country in Minnesota's Great North Woods.

This was Indian land in the most authentic sense, land that was never ceded, land that has never belonged to the United States. Aboriginal land held in common by its residents a la pre-reservation system. Red Lake is one of only two reservations to hold this unique sovereignty. At Red Lake - because of that distinction and its relative isolation - language, tradition and culture survive. Sovereignty, Red Lakers say, means sheltering traditions not as museum pieces for tourists, but as living expressions of what it means to be Indian.

I was on my way to Obaashiing (Windy Point). The community also known as Ponemah (a corruption of the Ojibwe Baanimaa meaning after a while or later) is at the western end of a peninsula that separates Upper and Lower Red Lake. This is the largest body of fresh water wholly contained within one state in the U.S. According to the 2000 census; Ponemah is the most Native American census location in the United Sates by percent. Obaashiing is 99.20% American Indian.

"Thus departed Hiawatha,

Hiawatha the Beloved,

In the glory of the sunset,

In the purple mists of evening,

To the regions of the home-wind,

Of the Northwest wind Keewaydin,

To the Islands of the Blessed,

To the kingdom of Ponemah,

To the land of the Hereafter!"

(From The Song of Hiawatha by Henry Wadsworth Longfellow)

Soon I arrived at the outskirts of this very Indian community known as the home of the Ojibwe language. If I was going anywhere else I'd be late, but when I entered this Indian land I was no longer on linear time, I was on Indian time. Time to the traditional Ojibwe unencumbered by "progress" is much more fluid than the time I was leaving behind. Time like almost everything in Ojibwe culture, is circular not linear.

The Healing Lodge was scheduled to begin at 9 a.m. and last until 4 p.m., but I knew that it would be closer to 9:30 or later by the time we got started. The temperature was in the high 70's to low 80's. The event, hosted on property under the stewardship of Larry and Violet Stillday, was billed as a Healing Lodge and Wellness Day for Providers. As is the custom at Red Lake, such an event would be cost free. Lunch would be provided as well as soft drinks, rolls, and coffee.

As I turned right off the reservation highway, I drove down a dirt road past a house on my left. There were two boys playing basketball in the yard. I kept going past the house and into the woods. Ahead I saw a few cars and a sign that said, "Welcome to Obaashiing University."

Somewhat to my surprise, there appears to be about 25 young non-Indians from Penn (Pennsylvania) State University. I am told they are in the area for two weeks studying Ojibwe culture, history, and language. They are being housed at Bemidji State University. This youth is balanced by perhaps twenty-five professional Red Lake members, most of who work for reservation social programs, New Beginnings, PATH, and Chemical Health.

The Web of Life

After a song by the *Wellbriety* Drum, a circle of sitting introductions ensued. Then our host and teacher for the day, Larry Stillday, asked those attending to stand and form a large circle. Violet Stillday produced a cat-sized ball of red yarn. Violet explained that she would throw the ball - unraveling as it flew - to another across the circle, and instructed that person to throw to another until a gigantic red web was formed.

The purpose of the exercise was to demonstrate the Web of Life and the tensions that can be created. Larry pointed out that when all held the yarn taut, the circle felt right, when most people raised their arms with the yarn while some did not, it destroyed the oneness and felt uncomfortable. Larry pointed out that we must work together in harmony. If one goes off on a drunk or other act averse to the group - because we are all connected - there is disharmony.

The Circle of Life (Medicine Wheel)

The next demonstration took place at the Medicine Wheel (also known as the Circle of Life). Larry asked all to gather around a large Medicine Wheel formed on the ground by birthday month and season. To the east would stand those with springtime birthdays, south summer, west autumn, and north winter. "Imagine a person who thinks they know it all," Larry said. "Not so. They look at the world only from their birthplace on the wheel. In order to know and understand, one must walk around the wheel, continually looking at the center, and notice how things look differently depending upon ones place on the wheel. We must walk the wheel to see how others see."

Notes & Larry Quotes

Balance and Harmony

- For balance and harmony, draw water with the flow, not against it.

- When we realize how we are connected, this leads to harmony. We must realize the connection of birth, death, and rebirth.

- There are four parts to us, mental, physical, emotional and spiritual. These must be in balance as well. We must have harmony in all four. If we do not, we are not well.

- We live in a balanced system, but it has two polarities. When conflict comes, it allows for change. We can make change. The Creator gives us stress and negative things to help us figure out what's wrong. It is a time for change, to do something more productive. Gossip, for example, leads to stress, stop it, and let it go. This will remove stress and anxiety. This is a problem of the world. If we have stress, we are out of balance and that will lead to even more stress.

The Spirit World

- There is a misunderstanding about Indians and spirits, we do not pray TO them, we pray FOR them.

- Evil will come. Don't say yes or no. That is an answer. If you answer, they then will have your power, you have given up your choice. Instead, keep walking.

- We are a diverse people. All our ceremonies are about man and woman. Where did you come from? The silly answer is from my mother and father. But this is true. Your mother and father are contained in you. You must therefore be balanced with the male and female. If you are not, you will be out of harmony and have stress. If you are a man and not in touch with the female, you cannot treat your woman right. We must balance the feminine with the masculine. If you neglect the feminine you will do the same with your partner. The switch around is also true.

Time

- Indians think in a circular rather than in a linear manner. That's why time seems less important, which is better for stress. Take things as they come.

- Why do some recognize a past separated from present time, which is, in turn, separated from the future? That is linear time. History is much more in the present for us.

- It is simple. The creator made it simple. There are lessons everywhere if we will but pay attention. We make it complicated. Get out of the way. Let life happen. We did not start on time. We did not finish a PowerPoint presentation. Something else happened that is just as...or more important. Questions were asked. Let it happen. Do not question such things, or let it cause you stress.

- To Indians, it is not so much about time as it is rhythm. Do not question what happens. Go with the flow.

The Red Road

- The Red Road is 18 inches long, from the mind to the heart.

- Being Indian is mainly in your heart. It's a way of walking with the earth instead of upon it. Many think about us Indians in the past tense, but we don't plan on going anywhere. We have lost much, but the thing that holds us together is that we all belong to and are protectors of our Earth Mother. That's the reason for us being here. Mother Earth is not a resource. She is life itself.

Tradition

- Indigenous or traditional knowledge has much to offer, e.g. environment, sustainable development, holistic healing, waste not.

- We must live in harmony. The Great Spirit works through Nature, that is why He is here, feel the connection. The two-legged, the four-legged and the winged ones are a part of nature. We are all connected. Each creature helps us understand. Everything is in the Sacred Hoop or Circle. As children and elders, and men and women can teach, so then can we learn from other living things. We have learned to fly by observation of creatures. They can see better, they can hear better, smell better. They may not be our equals in spirit, but they are our equals in nature. We must respect all life, they can teach.

The Sacred Circle

- The Sacred Circle of wellness. Live, love, respect, humility. Center on self. Ask the Great Spirit to come to your heart rather than your mind. This will remove stress and anxiety.

- Everything is a circle. There are no squares in nature. This equals unity, wholeness, birth and rebirth. We are still trying to figure out that human part, for we are spirits. The Creator teaches us through nature.

Teachings of the Seven Grandfathers

Among the Anishinaabe people, the Teachings of the Seven Grandfathers, also known simply as either the Seven Teachings or Seven Grandfathers, is a set of teachings on human conduct toward others. They are: Wisdom, Love, Respect, Bravery or Courage, Honesty, Humility, and Truth.

Background

According to the *aadizookaan* (sacred stories), the teachings were given to the Anishinaabeg early in their history. Seven Grandfathers asked their messenger to take a survey of the human condition. At that time the human condition was not very good. Eventually in his quest, the messenger came across a child. After receiving approval from the Seven Grandfathers, the messenger tutored the child in the "Good way of Life". Before departing from the Seven Grandfathers, each of the Grandfathers instructed the child with a principle.

Niizhwaaso Mishoomis Gikinoo'amaagewwinnaan

(The Seven Grandfathers Teachings)

- **Nibwaakaawin (Wisdom):** To cherish knowledge is to know Wisdom. Wisdom is given by the Creator to be used for the good of the people. This word expresses not only wisdom, but also prudence, or intelligence. This word can also mean intelligence or knowledge.

- **Zaagi'idiwin (Love):** To know Love is to know peace. Love must be unconditional. When people are weak they need love the most. The word also indicates that this form of love is mutual.

- **Minwaadendamowin (Respect):** To honor all creation is to have Respect. All of creation must be treated with respect. If you wish to be respected, you must give respect.

- **Aakwade'ewin (Bravery/Courage):** Bravery is to face a foe with integrity. This word literally means "state of having a fearless heart" in Ojibwemowin. We must do what is right even when the consequences are unpleasant.

- **Gwekowaadiziwin (Honesty):** Honesty in facing a situation is to be brave. Always be honest in word and action. Be honest first with yourself, and you will more easily be able to be honest with others. This word can also mean righteousness.

- **Dabaadendiziwin (Humility)**: Humility is to know yourself as a sacred part of Creation. This word can also mean compassion. You are equal to others, but you are not better. Some may interpret this concept as calmness, meekness, gentility or patience in addition to humility.

- **Debwewin (Truth)**: Truth is to know all of these things. Speak the truth. Do not deceive yourself in particular or others.

The PowerPoint Teaching was not finished, but questions were answered and the hour near supper, when Violet handed out diplomas for completing the day's Teaching at Obaashiing University.

And as we began to prepare to head south, back to our linear world, we heard Gichi-Ma'iingan say, "Gigaagiigidotamaagoom, maada'ooyok gaa-mi-inigooyeg". "You are speakers for us now, share what you have learned."

Healing Lodges/Wellness Days

Larry and Violet Stillday hosted what they referred to as a Healing Lodge and/or Wellness Day, a total of five times at Obaashiing University. You have just read about the first. What follows are my notes on the next three of four Lodges.

Healing Lodge 2 took place in August 2010. I have misplaced or did not take notes for Healing Lodge 3 held July 2011. For Healing Lodge 4 in August 2012, I took notes again. The last, Healing Lodge 5, was held July 23, 2013. This was also the day of my Naming Ceremony. That Healing Lodge, in print as it was in life, preludes my Naming Ceremony story.

August 31, 2010, Notes from a Healing Lodge #2

"There are those who wish to copy our Sweat, our Naming Ceremonies, and now our Teachings. Now people ask to use them. That's what it is for, it is for our Earth Mother." ~Gichi-Ma'iingan

The *Wellbriety* Drum was present. The Drum was a gift from White Bison, an organization that Larry and Violet respected. White Bison teaches that,

"Healing will take place through the application of cultural and spiritual knowledge."

All guests introduced themselves and spoke briefly as to why they were present and what they hoped to get out of the Teaching. Many introduced themselves speaking their Spirit names in Ojibwemowin.

Balance and Harmony

- When you say you can't, you hold yourself hostage.

- Ojibwe is an active or verb based language. It is hard to find a word that means I can't.

- Conflict and struggle always goes to light. It is an evolving system. This is a part of life. It is a friend. Conflict results in fight or flight. When conflict starts it's time to get happy, because some change is going to occur, the Elders say.

Mother Earth

- We need to get in the rhythm of nature, for in nature there is balance. Sometimes we find ourselves swimming upstream. We spend a lot of energy swimming this way. We must follow the natural order and go with the flow. Color outside the lines like a child. Don't get stuck in the rules.

- We are never alone in the woods.

- Bring to one's mind and honor our Earth Mother, then to honor the lake, water, and the four directions. They don't need us.

- What do you do if your mate is to give birth? I'd be there to hold her hand, to wipe her brow. This is your Mother. Take care of her.

The Physical World

- The Physical world relies on the five senses. Be careful, we might get stuck there. When we do that it excludes the Spiritual, which we need for more balance.

- We must possess a willingness to change. We must think about it and then act. Our leaders will follow wherever the community leads.

- If we get stuck in the physical world, we think, well at least we are good for something.

The Red Road

- The Red Road equals growth. The Cycle of Life is blueprint. The eight Development Stages are, Trust, Autonomy, Initiative, Accomplishment, Identity, Intimacy, Generosity, and Integrity.

The Sacred Circle

- There are four laws of change. Change comes from within. Ceremonies help you center, to quiet your mind.

- Direction of Healing; individual, family, community then responds, then Nation.

- Who are your parents? Who do you spend time with? My father? You neglect your mother. You are unbalanced. We need to connect the male to the female.

- I dedicate myself to my sanctuary, to keep balance. How we are interconnected.

- The Creator put everything in a circle for us. We need to walk. Everything is there.

The Seven Teachings

- We must practice the Seven Teachings. They are Love, represented by the Bald Eagle or Migizi. Migizi teaches love and balance. Beaver or Amik represents Wisdom. Bear or Makwa represents Courage. Makwa is a sentry and is gentle. Makwa knows all medicine. When a bear gets hurt it goes to the medicine.

- Mashkode-Bizhiki or Buffalo/Bison represents Respect, Mikinaak or Snapping Turtle Truth, Ma'iingan or Wolf, Humility, and Misaabe or Bigfoot, Honesty.

- Animals teach us things. They never broke their relationship with the plants and so they know the medicine.

Smudging

- Smudging, using abalone shells, represents the four elements. Fire smoke symbolizes Air. Earth is represented by the medicine plant sage. The abalone shell symbolizes Water. In this way we bring a balance of the elements.

- The embers in the sage bundle need a fan to keep them burning. Some consider it disrespectful to blow on the smudge with one's breath. A hand may be used to fan the embers, but a feather, or feather fan, are more effective.

The Spirit World

- Remember, you were born into a world already broken. We must meditate daily using the Seven Directions. Each day you start with a clean slate. If you have a bad day, at night give it to the Manidoog (Spirits). Say, "I give it to you grandfather." Live moment to moment. Our task is service to the Creator.

The Sweat Lodge

After the Teachings, for those who wished to stay, a sweat lodge would be held at 6 p.m. after the Wellness Lodge.

This was my first Sweat Lodge. Swimsuits and towels were provided for those who did not expect to sweat or forgot. Three hand drums played a song while a fire was built and rocks placed on the fire. Soon, several men and women entered the sweat in a clocklike direction crawling on hands and knees, Larry spoke more of the Sweat Lodge.

The Sweat has four doors or phases. There are nineteen stones, seven for the Seven Directions, and then with each following of three phases, four more heated rocks would be added. If it gets too hot or uncomfortable, please take care of you, and withdraw. You may reenter at any phase. The Sacred Path, from the fire to the Sweat, does not get crossed once the fire is lit. Rocks are only used once. The spent or split rock is then piled and symbolizes the moon.

- There are those who wish to copy our Sweat, our Naming Ceremonies, and now our Teachings. Now people ask to use them. That's what it is for, it is for our Earth Mother.

I won't describe the experience, as Larry would caution me that ceremony couldn't be read about. It must be experienced. "That's the reason the old people didn't write down much of the information, because it was turned around and translated in a linear way, which it then lost its' major content and purpose."

Tradition & Heritage

- The kindling of the 8th Fire (Seven Fires Prophecy) comes from here and other places, "ripples are sent out."

- There is an urgency to get young people involved as the elders are getting sick and passing on.

July 26, 2011, Notes from a Healing Lodge #3

But you know, it doesn't bother me at all. I've been to Ponemah!

Though I have misplaced my notes (so no quotes) from the day or took none, I do remember some of what I saw and learned.

A bus came in from a tribal treatment center made up of mostly teenage girls. Though there were more adults than youth, Larry geared much of his teachings that day to reflect issues that might benefit the young women. That included peeling away more layers of the Medicine Wheel.

He spoke of the five sacred gifts, our senses, and how they aid us in learning to be human. He spoke of ceremony and the order of creation; minerals, plants, animals, and then humans.

We discussed the Eight Stages of Development or Stages of Life; Trust, Autonomy, Initiative, Accomplishment, Identity, Intimacy, Generosity, and Integrity.

Larry told us that if we missed going through any of these stages, that they don't go away, they are still there until we go through it. And so we walk the wheel. He said it started when we were told as young children not to color outside the lines. It's okay to color outside the lines.

Larry often said that we are not humans learning to be spiritual, but are spirits learning to be human. The Creator gave us different but related tools to aid in that endeavor. In learning to be human, the five senses work with all four aspects of being.

The Four Aspects of Being: The physical (body) and mental (mind) aspects are part of the "seen" world, and emotional (heart) and spiritual (soul) aspects are part of the "unseen" world. We often concentrate on the seen and ignore the unseen or hidden. To learn to be human, the Four Aspects however must all be in balance. A person cannot neglect one or two to the detriment of the others.

Many think of the sacred gifts of the five senses as affecting only the body and mind. It seems our five senses are often distracted by the "seen" (mind and body) to the detriment and neglect of the "unseen" (spirit and heart). We sometimes forget that the senses also sense the unseen. Can we deny the scent of a flower, the sight of a beautiful sunset, the sound of music, the taste of honey, or the touch of a child affects the heart and soul?

If we are not in balance with all four aspects we feel stress, and stress in response makes us sick physically, mentally, emotionally and spiritually.

We learn these things by practicing the four P's, Purpose, Prayer, Perseverance and Passion.

August 16, 2012, Notes from a Healing Lodge #4

"Made as comfortable as possible, humans complicate the simplest thing." ~Gichi-Ma'iingan

A notice was sent to those interested, *"Healing Lodge, August 16, 2012, 9 am until 4 pm. Sweat Lodge at 6 pm. at Larry's Healing Lodge in Ponemah.*

We're having chili and salad for lunch, we'll welcome chips, cookies or donuts if

*you'd like to bring something. We'll also have coffee, water and lemonade. Invite family, friends, and neighbors. **Every one is welcome***.

Please respond if you're coming so we'll have an idea of the number of attendees.

Please let me know if you have any questions. Hope to see you then.

Chi-miigwech!! Violet Stillday."

Balance and Harmony

Having no agenda awakes your innate knowledge. Tap into each other. Innate or indigenous knowledge will lead to balance and harmony.

There are Seven Laws about How to be Human. Love, Respect, Bravery, Wisdom, Honesty, Truth, Humility.

Ceremony

We are not here to learn about how to become spirits, but to become human. We come from the spirit. The Creator gave us ceremony to teach us how to be human. Ceremony is about how to be human.

Ceremony: All that is life is in the Medicine Wheel.

There are Four Visions: Prayer, Purpose, Perseverance, and Passion.

There are Two Aspects: the Seen World, which is physical and mental, and the Unseen World, which is emotional and spiritual.

Mother Earth

We all have this blueprint. Go to nature.

Some do not like to be who they are. Who am I? The Creator gave us the five senses as gifts, to learn how to be in the physical world. These are known

as the Five Sacred Gifts.

We needed solids first to build that rock foundation, the mineral people, then the plant people, animals then humans. The four elements, Earth, Fire, Water, and Air. We can't live without these families.

Snake teaches us to walk left to right. We cannot walk in a straight line. Veer left to right.

The Stages of Life

There are Eight Stages of Life described below: numbers 1 to 4, refer to life between babe to youth, 5 and 6, describe youth to adult, and 7 and 8 refer to adult and elder. (If there was a violation there will be trouble with number 5)

1. Trust = as a newborn

2. Autonomy = I am someone, I can do it

3. Initiative = active imagination

4. Accomplishment = good at being a person

5. Identity = validation, who am I, why am I here, where am I going

6. Intimacy = sexualize, able to relate to the world

7. Generosity = giving and accepting

8. Integrity = walks the talk, understanding, wisdom

July 23, 2013, Notes from a Healing Lodge #5

"I was so afraid of wood-ticks 'til I learned I could outrun them." ~Gichi-Ma'iin-gan

Notes & Larry Quotes

Balance and Harmony

You made me do it? Take responsibility. We are responsible for ourselves.

Tired of hurting? Looking for Spirit? Do you breathe? Spirit first, we have the teachings inside of us. Don't walk a straight line. We walk in circles many times during the day.

Walk the physical life. The Creator gave us the five senses as tools.

Perception, this is where I see from.

Ceremony

When we smudge, we are saying Miigwech; we are using all the four elements.

A Pipe Ceremony is about bringing the male/female together, to connect.

Look for spirit guides and animal helpers.

In the East, look for love and eagle.

In the South, look for loyalty and wolf

In the West, look for introspection, vision quest and bear.

In the North, look for generosity and buffalo.

The Medicine Wheel

The Medicine Wheel beginning in the East going clockwise, financial, occupational, social, and environmental.

The Seven Laws are in the four directions. The Four Sacred Medicines are Tobacco, Cedar, Sage, and Sweet Grass.

Sacred Medicines in the Medicine Wheel

East = tobacco, spiritual, male, fire, spirit, baby

South = cedar, emotional, feminine, water, emotion, youth

West = sage, masculine, earth, physical, adult

North = sweet grass, feminine, air, mental, elder

We move in a circle. We must move about the Medicine Wheel to experience nature, we are related. Nature doesn't need us; we need nature. We are all related. Say a short prayer. Miigwech is a prayer.

When you start your journey, do it in a circle. Every revolution brings clarity. I learn every time I listen to this. The world repeats.

Mother Earth

You awake to innate knowledge. Where we come from, and who we are. The four elements, we are of the earth, we are these elements. The trees clean the air so we can breathe. We need to take care of them.

Wellness

Wellness, how we get it? We must know what we are looking for. We are in the presence of our elders. Go to that place within when it is quiet. The Vision

I had from above the two lakes, they looked like lungs and so this lodge is placed between the lungs, at the heart, at Ponemah.

Wellness includes more than the physical, it also includes mental, emotional, and spiritual. Are balance, harmony and peace within not constant? But there is a new awareness, pay attention to yourself. Think about what you are thinking about.

Wellness is not a word; it's how you feel.

"Practice Non-interference. I will walk with you. If we miss it, we don't go back, we keep going in the circle and pick it up on the next round. ~Gichi-Ma'iingan

July 23 will always be a special anniversary for me. It was on that day that Gichi-Ma'iingan: Gaa-izhinikaanid (Big Wolf: The One Who Named Me) presided over a Waawiindaasowin (Naming Ceremony) at the close of his last "Healing Lodge" held at "Obaashiing University." It was a special day.

June 10, 2014, Notes from a Healing Lodge #6 Never to Be

The Sixth Wellness Lodge had been scheduled for June 10, 2014. Larry turned 70 on May 14, and died on May 20, 2014.

On May 20, 2014, at 9:09 a.m., Jen Kruse, a close friend of Larry Stillday, Jr., wrote in "private message" on Facebook. "Are you there?" (I was sleeping)

At 9:21 a.m. she wrote again. "Michael, Larry Stillday, Sr., passed away in his sleep last night. It was not expected. Larry, Jr., and I are heading up there this afternoon. I thought you should be told instead of just finding out in a news-feed or something. I don't have your phone number or I would have called instead."

At 10:27 a.m. I see the message. "No, no, no! No," I cried, "please tell me it's not the man who gave me my name."

At 12:03 p.m. Jen writes again. "This morning - after we received the news, I was hugging Larry, Jr., and we were weeping over losing him, and then I saw him when I closed my eyes, he said, 'Just keep walking.'"

I spent most of the day speaking with friends about Larry's death. At 6:59 p.m., I wrote back to Jen, "That gives me some comfort. I have heard him say this very thing on several occasions, that when we meet some unpleasantness to 'just keep walking it may look different the next time around or not, but just keep walking.' I can't tell you how grateful I am that you contacted me personally, it is a big deal, you are right. I would have hated to read it on Facebook or on the radio, or from anyone else really. Thank you so much."

Lawrence Edward Stillday, Sr.
(May 14, 1944 - May 20, 2014)

As is the Indian custom, a 24-hour a day wake was held beginning on Saturday, May 24. Traditional Services would commence at 1:00 pm Monday, May 26, 2014, all held at the Ponemah Boys and Girls Club in Ponemah. Interment was at the family burial grounds in Ponemah.

For weeks, those of us who had participated in past Healing Lodges communicated through email, social media and by phone. Many of us shared our feelings of a heavy heart and deep sadness, but we also shared memories of wisdom and humor. We talked about attending the 6th Healing Lodge anyway as Larry hadn't cancelled it. Larry might like that. Many of us trickled into Obaashiing University during the day of June 10. There was nothing formal, nothing organized, just walking through the woods of Obaashiing University in reflection. We just kept walking.

Part 2

Nin-Waawiindaasowin
(My Naming Ceremony)

"Thus, deeply affected by an Ojibwa naming ceremony he attended in May of 1809, he later recorded his admiration for these Indians 'without the Slightest, most distant instruction in the knowledge of Divine Truths, should still have such ideas of human obligations and express them with such beautiful Simplicity and not infrequently with Sublimity of expression that would do honor to many of our clergy.'" ~ George Nelson, The Orders of the Dreamed, intro: page 23

Preparation Lead-up to Ceremony

Opening Narrative:

You've probably guessed by now that I have interest and respect for American Indigenous culture. I thought it was kind of cool when I'd hear that some non-Indian was "adopted" by a tribe, but I was more attracted to the idea of being given a Spirit (Indian) name. I didn't really know all that much about either one.

What follows is the story about how I came to get an Ojibwe Spirit name. Respectfully, Biidaanakwad Indizhinikaaz! (Gathering Cloud is My Name) Bemijigamaag Indoonjibaa. (Bemidji is my home) This, with the addition of clan membership, is a common way to introduce oneself in Ojibwemowin.

How it Began

In May 2013, I had just begun fasting for 72 hours every other week. Basically I started for weight loss. I haven't lost that much weight, but it makes me feel good and has many benefits beyond physical. I have thought about "spirit quests" from time-to-time since coming into contact with Indian culture. At this time I was remembering the good things many religions and spiritual people have said about the benefits of fasting.

Larry taught that we are not human beings learning how to be spiritual, but spiritual beings learning how to be human. We were given the five senses to help us achieve this. We also must maintain a balance in all we do, including the four aspects of self: spirit, heart, mind and body.

To aid us in this endeavor of learning to be human, we were given Seven Principles or Seven Teachings by the Creator to help us attain Mino-bimaa-diziwin (The Good Life or Wellness). These Seven Gifts are love, respect, truth, wisdom, courage, honesty, and humility. These gifts must be practiced equally, also kept in balance, favoring none over another.

Therefore, when Larry spoke of healing or good health or wellness, he wasn't just talking about the body, but all four aspects of being. A person cannot neglect one to the benefit of another and still maintain wellness. This is not religion in the western sense then, but more than religion, it is a way of life. The spiritual is not compartmentalized. The four aspects are one. All exist as a whole. All are related. All must be in balance. These are the teachings of the Midewiwin sometimes translated as Grand Medicine Society, the "religion" or "way of life" of the traditional and historic Ojibwe.

Likewise then, when speaking of medicine or Medicine People, we are speaking of medicine in its broadest sense and healing for all four aspects of self, spirit, heart, mind and body.

Ceremony is important for all people. It's an important symbol that marks and celebrates transitions or changes in life. The dominant culture, in a general sense, seem to have forgotten this, minimized it, trivialized it, or cast it aside to our detriment in my view. I add these observations to the narrative to demonstrate that the naming ceremony has substance and meaning. It is not a pat on the head for being a good White boy or a pal to Indians.

What follows is a chronicle beginning with the first contact I made with Larry in mid- March 2013, which eventually culminated with my naming ceremony on July 23, 2013. This is a four-month period. The number four holds significance in the Teachings of the Medicine Wheel.

On March 14, 2013 I wrote to Larry Stillday: "I seem to be in a searching mode of late, perhaps my age. I have been reading Carl Jung, looking at the more mystical parts of our major religions, the Gnostics, Kabbalah, and Buddhism. I have also been reviewing my notes on your words. What you teach is not much different from what I've been reading, and the similarities astounded me for a moment, but not for long. What you teach has the added benefit of being local, of being ours, and perhaps being more user friendly. That Medicine Wheel seems to be quite the teaching tool."

Larry replied: "Hey niiji, (my friend) good to hear from you. You sound like you're way out in the woods, which is not a bad place to be when you're wondering about life in general.

"You know the Creator gave all people the same instructions. That's why he put the four colors of people on the medicine wheel, including the gifts he bestowed on each race. So it's no surprise to me that it would have a lot of similarities, the teachings are more about our similarities then our differences.

"From what I hear is that you are ready to embark on an inward journey. If you agree I would be honored to take you to the threshold of your journey, if you want."

I didn't yet realize the significance of his offer, but perhaps unconsciously I did. He does not mention a "naming" and I didn't interpret it that way. It's only in hindsight, going through these old emails nearly two years later, that I see he offered something quite special. It is only as I write this narrative that I realize the full impact possible of such an offer by such a teacher.

Two days later I wrote back mentioning that the dark days of winter were depressing me a bit. "I am ready to embark on an inward journey. It pleases me greatly that you are willing to 'take me to the threshold of that journey.' An honor indeed! Perhaps I will contact you even soon in that regard. I am unsure how to begin such a journey."

Larry replied: "You know the weather has a tendency to affect people many different ways. That's because it is a good teacher. We just need to listen to the lessons. In other words, we align ourselves to the lessons. The first lesson the seasons teach us is alignment.

You ask how to prepare for the journey, getting yourself aligned is where to begin."

May 2013, Two months later (mid-May during an email thread) an acquaintance of mine and a friend of the Larry Stillday family, asked if I had an Indian (Spirit) name and if not why not. I told her that I had thought of it from time to time, but I really didn't know how to go about it. She said to write Larry, tell him that you feel you are ready to move forward on your journey, and then ask how to go about receiving an Indian name. She was confident he would reply in the positive.

He did. Later she said to bring him tobacco and ask again, which I did at a language revitalization celebration at Ponemah in mid-June.

On May 21, 2013 I wrote Larry about a Spirit name. "I am feeling willing and ready to move forward in my Journey. Would you share with me what I should do, to ask for and/or prepare for, a spirit name indaga? (Please) Also, when the time is right, I would like to learn more of, and at some point do, a Vision Quest."

"So you are feeling ready to advance on your journey," Larry wrote back, "that's good. The next time we meet we will sit down and talk about the preparation."

"I look forward to meeting with you on preparation to advance on my journey," I answered. "I am pleased and honored to have a willing teacher such as you. Thank you so much."

On June 25, 2013 I wrote a letter of eulogy on the passing of a friend, Gary Fuller, and sent it to several mutual friends.

Larry wrote back, "Sorry of the news of another loss for us as a people. How are you doing my friend? Let me know if there's anything I can do."

"I hope we can get together soon," I replied. "I have had many challenges of late. I feel it is time for me to move forward on my journey. I seek your guidance."

"Sorry to hear of your difficulties," Larry answered. "You know as human beings we all go through certain things that are very much similar to all, no nationality, race or creed is exempt from human experiences. Yes, we must get together soon."

He then mentions a language revitalization event to be held at the Ponemah powwow grounds on the next day's eve. "There's a calling to all community members. Hope you would be able to come," he wrote. (Something always compelled me to attend whatever whenever he invited me in such a manner.)

"I will be there tomorrow," I said. "Perhaps we could chat a bit before or after the event?"

Larry wrote the next morning confirming that evening's event but he didn't answer my question. "It's a go," I wrote back. "Will you have time for me tonight or should we put off 'til a better time or when the time is right? I still apparently have trouble knowing when the time is right. Little excited I guess, something I've thought about for years hoping I was 'worthy.'"

"Yeah we can talk some this evening, there are questions I need to ask," Larry answered. "Then we will look at the time to have the ceremony and where. See you there."

Asemaa (Tobacco)

I'd been around Indians long enough to know the very important daily role that asemaa (tobacco) plays as a Sacred medicine in the culture of the Ojibwe. It is used in a variety of ways as a symbol of humility, respect, and gratefulness to the Creator and all of creation, even to a certain degree among Christians.

Protocol dictated that I present Larry with tobacco to begin this process as a formal request. If Larry accepted the tobacco, he was then bound to fulfill that request.

Just before driving to Ponemah to attend the language revitalization event, I cut a piece of red cloth into a 4 x 4 inch square. I also cut from the same cloth a 6 inch strip a quarter inch wide to use as a tie. I then placed a pipe-full of tobacco into the center of the square and tied it so I had a little red bundle of asemaa that looked a bit like a large Hershey's Kiss.

While attending the Ponemah language event I was kind of nervous not knowing exactly when or…in a way…how, to present the tobacco. Toward the end of the gathering, I presented Larry the tobacco asking if he would instruct me in how to prepare for a Spirit name, and he accepted it. Although I was expecting some kind of preparation instructions or questions as he'd mentioned earlier, something told me he was tired and it was too late in the evening. This bothered me a bit. I was being impatient.

By the way, among the Red Lake Ojibwe, tobacco is held with the left hand (closest to the heart) by both the giver and receiver. But there is really no wrong way to give tobacco.

But because it plays such a major role in this culture, allow me to digress and give you a couple paragraphs on tobacco as a symbol and Sacred Medicine.

"Tobacco, among the Ojibwe, is used for prayers of gratitude to thank the Creator for our many blessings. When any plant is picked or an animal taken, tobacco and prayer is given as a sign of respect and gratefulness. By honoring all our relations we demonstrate that we have not forgotten our place within the web of life.

To offer someone tobacco is to ask that you and the person receiving the tobacco be of one heart, one mind, one spirit and you have the same purpose. Tobacco is offered when you ask someone to do a ceremony for you, such as a naming ceremony, a smudging, sweat lodge; any ceremony.

Tobacco is given to elders and others when seeking advice. It shows gratitude and respect for the person whose advice you are seeking. Tobacco is given when you appreciate a teaching from an elder, or even a younger person, if you value what that person has told you." ~Excerpted from The Sacred Use of Tobacco by Alex Fergusson in Psychology Today.2013

On June 26, 2013, at that evening's language powwow at Ponemah, I offered Larry tobacco asking him to conduct a naming ceremony at some future date.

Some two weeks later, and with only a weeks' notice, Larry, in an email exchange, eventually let me know when the naming ceremony would be and what I needed to do in preparation.

Larry wrote on July 12, 2013, "Hey niiji, (my friend) I finally set the date for the Wellness Day. It's going to be on July 23rd, Tuesday, 9 am to 4:30. The theme will be "What is wellness?" (He mentions nothing of a naming ceremony.)

I wrote back, "I'll be there. I'm sure Barry will come too, not sure if wife

Barb can get off work."

Three days later Larry wrote: "Hey niiji, yeah Barry said he'll be there. (Been) working out there (Wellness Lodge site) today had some wind damage from the storm Friday night. Three pretty good size trees were blown down, so that's what I was doing this morning. Just about got it all cleared out. We are going to put up a canopy, actually it's a carport, going to try to do PowerPoint again."

I wrote back: "Sounds like hard work cutting up trees. We got wind down here, but not like you got up there. Barb may be coming, she just has to check with work tomorrow, they let her come last time on their dime, figured she might learn something about Indians ;-)."

Showing my impatience again, I wrote; "Do I need to remind you about the "naming" or will you bring it up 'when the time is right'?"

I added a PS, "I'm happy to say that Barb is able to come. Later, I'm tired."

Larry wrote; "I hope you're not sleeping yet, but what I want to say is, I hope she lets you come too."

"I was sleeping," I wrote a few hours later. "She has now gone to bed. I'll check, yes I hope she lets me come too. Honestly, I've been eager to move on. I'll work on patience. It has not been one of my virtues."

Now I get my first hint that a naming ceremony will take place when I get a note back from Larry the next morning, now about a week out.

"Sounds good, I do hope she will let you come," he wrote. "I would like to have you bring a fruit dish, it can be strawberries, blueberries, or raspberries. You can add banana, or watermelon, and if you can bring a wild rice hot dish, we will use that for the naming ceremony."

His words still seemed unclear leaving me unsure yet hopeful the ceremony was for me.

A few days later and only two days out, somewhat to my surprise, Larry told me by phone, that I needed to identify at least two "sponsors" or we'enh's. (I could have four or even eight)

Not knowing for sure who would attend, the first folks that came to mind were the only two people I knew would be there for sure. So I submitted the names of my wife Barbara and my good friend Barry. (In hindsight I can't think of two better people. They are among my closest friends, and also have high interest and respect for this culture.)

A little uneasiness swept over me for a moment. It occurred to me that they both were White, neither was Indian. So I asked awkwardly, "Wait, or do I need a couple of Indian sponsors?"

This is the first of several times I heard Larry utter this mater-of-fact, no-need-for-more-questions statement that defined his wisdom as a great teacher, in my view. Larry said, and said no more, "It's not about Indians, it's about people." The teachings were for everyone and anyone and he said that often and in many ways. I indeed felt like a student.

The We-enh Responsibility

We'enh is short for Niiyawe'enh (My Namesake or sponsor or guardian; similar to godparents. Plural would be Niiyawe'enhyag. The life-long we-enh role is to advise, and watch over their namesake. The named may always go to any we-enh, and they will take time to listen or offer advice.

"The person who gives the name and the sponsors who witness are really the same. They all witness. They all sponsor. They all act like godparents. In Ojibwe, they are also all called niiyawe'enh (my namesake). In third person they are called wiiyawe'enyan (his namesake). They can all be called we'enh or we' or niiyawe' for short." ~Dr. Anton Treuer, Professor of Ojibwe, Bemidji State University

The day before the Healing Lodge, and what I now assumed would include a Naming Ceremony for me, I wrote to Larry. "Will there be a generator at Obaashiing University tomorrow? Trying to decide how to keep wild rice dish hot."

"Boozhoo," wrote Larry, "yes there will be a generator running. We will be setting up hopefully around 8 am if not exactly somewhere shortly after that time. Will be seeing you."

I wrote back with anticipation, "Can you remind me the word you used for 'sponsor' or 'godparent? Is there somewhere I can look and learn a bit more about what is happening? Or is that not necessary? I'm very much looking forward to this. I am honored and flattered. I should be honored and flattered right? I feel like I should know more."

Impatient again, and wanting to know more about the ceremony in which I was to participate, I spent some time researching on the internet. I wrote Larry again.

"I searched, for that is my nature - I am curious. Good thing I am not a gaazhagens (cat). We-enh is the word translating as guardian? I am honored and flattered to the point of tears…not sure exactly why. I have prepared a gift of tobacco for my two Niiyawe'enhyag, Barbara and Barry."

Larry wrote his last email of the night on July 22, 2013. As was his manner, he wrote back in such a way, which was gentle, respectful and wise yet made feel again like I had a long way to go, or that somehow I should have already known this. His words also lifted me up, excited for what lay ahead for me as a student of such a teacher.

"Hey, when one first starts off on their personal journey, it is very common that one wants to know what lies ahead. That's common and that's human nature.

When I guide people, since it's their journey, I don't know what lies ahead of them. But what happens is as they walk, they take me to the gifts that lie on their path, and that's when and how I will interpret for them that which they come upon. Only the Creator knows what He put in place for each individual.

The name for god/parent or namesake is wiiyawe'enh, (my namesake). Now that you begin your journey you will learn more."

Every time I read these words I wonder what might have been.

Naming Day Eve

After the last email from Larry, somehow it came to me that I should write Indaanisag (my daughters) Kimberly Irene and Erin Marie to let them know of my naming ceremony coming the next day. I explained that it happened so fast I could not let them know sooner in case they might want to come. They both responded in such a way that you would know they are my daughters.

That same night, the eve of the Naming Ceremony, Barbara and I made our first ever wild rice hot dish as a team to be served the next day. We had two recipes but made it our own. At one point we thought we screwed up with too much water, but somehow it turned out to be tastily creative rather than a mistake.

When it comes to cooking and partnerships, it was a classic example of "the whole being greater than the sum of its parts." All agreed later that it was delicious. Barbara also made up a fruit dish of various types of berries as Larry had instructed, all for which I am grateful.

This was an atypical occurrence, and from my view, was the beginning of 24 hours of unusual things.

The Day of Ceremony

Obaashiing University

About 7:10 a.m. on July 23, 2013, Barbara and I mounted the mustang. We traveled north on Irvine or County #15, past the continental divide at Buena Vista, past the farmlands of Nebish to the woodlands of the Red Lake Indian Reservation. Shortly after entering this land that was never ceded, Migizi (bald eagle) flew overhead. Later Waagosh (fox) sat along the west side of the road looking east watching us pass.

Shortly after crossing State Hwy. #1, dotting the edge of the tree line, artistic rendered wooden signs warned of the dangers of alcohol along with, "Welcome to Ponemah, and Home of the Ojibway Language." Ojibwe speakers know Ponemah, another 20 miles down the road, as Obaashiing.

Red Lake, mostly Ponemah, has more fluent Ojibwe speakers than the rest of the US combined, although there are many in Canada. A Christian church has yet to survive in the community. Ponemah, because of its isolation combined with tribe's unique status, language, culture and tradition survive here perhaps like nowhere else outside the southwest.

Soon we reached the outskirts of Obaashiing. The Ojibwe, like many other Indigenous Peoples, truly have a different concept of time and place. Deep into traditional Indian land, we were no longer on linear time, but on Indian time (circular as opposed to linear). The Healing Lodge was scheduled to begin at 9 a.m. but we knew it might be closer to 9:30 by the time we got started.

Traditional Indians just accept, as a matter of good manners, that cultural events in particular will begin when they're supposed to begin. They don't really question it or get upset by such things as being on time. They accept that there must be a reason, or perhaps even a lesson to be learned, probably directed by the Creator and therefore not to be questioned.

The temperature was in the 70's. The event, hosted on property under the stewardship of Larry and Violet Stillday, was billed as a Healing Lodge and Wellness Day. As is the custom at Red Lake, the event would be cost free.

Nearing the community of Ponemah, we took a right off the reservation highway into a driveway. To our right were Spirit Houses. Many Ponemah residents who still practice the old ways bury their relatives on the home property. They build these little houses to cover the grave. They are as long and wide as a grave, but only a foot or two high. We continued to drive down a dirt road past a house on our left and into the woods.

Ahead we saw a few cars and a partial clearing. We must have been among the first to arrive. According to the time stamp on the photos, it was just after 8:00 a.m. Larry was hanging a welcome sign and we stopped to help. We chuckled, the sign read, "Welcome to Obahshiing (sic) University."

We brought our food gifts to homemade tables to be eaten later. Here we placed the fruit dish, but the wild rice dish we placed at a table a bit further away to plug into a relatively quiet generator. We were not told nor did we guess that our food should be kept separate, so the wild rice was fine, the fruit maybe not.

Barry, wife Linda and granddaughter Kiley Mae arrived soon after. I took this opportunity, before the start, to give asemaa wrapped in a small red cloth bundle (as I did Larry the month before) to Barbara and Barry and thanked each for acting as my we'enh.

Larry's teaching that day centered on the Gifts of the Seven Grandfathers and touched on the many layers of the Medicine Wheel. All during the day, the naming ceremony was not mentioned and I was unsure that it would.

Perhaps only twenty to twenty-five people attended the Wellness Lodge, mostly from the Chemical Health and Women's Shelter programs, and some of Larry's relatives.

Most attendees left at the end of the day, about 3:30 pm, either not knowing of, or not interested in, the naming ceremony to come. Larry did not announce it, but rather, let whatever happens, happen. Two women friends, Stephanie and Darlene, asked what was going on and decided to stay.

Again, traditional Indians really do seem to have an attitude of acceptance of the way things are and often when something happens unexpected, will accept and even assign meaning to the change in plans ultimately coming as a message of sorts from the Creator.

All the women donned Ceremonial skirts. I don't know what to compare it to other than maybe the Catholic Church's past tradition of women wearing some kind of head covering during mass when I was young. They are long, often with colorful prints.

I have been told that many traditional women keep them handy and wear them for any number of ceremonies. Often they are put on over whatever else they are wearing just for the time of the ceremony. If someone unfamiliar with the custom has arrived "skirt-less," the host women might have a dozen or more skirts to loan to those without.

A near glitch happened when we discovered our fruit dish had disappeared during lunch. The dish was to be part of the ceremony. Larry calmly asked his sister Rose if there were fruits left from the lunch. There were. He then asked her to make up a fruit dish from those leftovers, which she did.

In addition to Larry and myself, those in attendance included my we'enh's Barb and Barry, Linda, Kiley Mae, Larry's wife Violet, his older sister Rose, her daughter (Larry's niece) Vickey, and our two women friends who decided to stay, Stephanie and Darlene.

Larry took a seat in a lawn chair facing west at the northeast corner of a small square table, which earlier had been used for Medicine Wheel teachings. But now on the table, were the gifts Barbara and I had brought, the wild rice hot-dish and the fruit bowl that Larry's sister Rose made up to replace the one eaten at lunch.

Larry then gave directions.

Barb and Barry were to sit next to each other on a picnic bench to the south. Barry was to Barb's left. I sat in a lawn chair opposite Larry facing east at the northwest corner of the table. As in all things ceremonial, there is symbolic significance to the directions in which we all sat. I was facing east where the day begins. Violet, Vickey and Rose sat to the north opposite Barb and Barry to the south. The women would be helpers of sorts. We occupied the four quadrants. Linda, Kiley, Stephanie and Darlene sat in the east behind Larry facing me.

Meanwhile, Rose bent over the low table to my right and in front of Larry, who was preparing a spirit dish.

A spirit dish is made up of small portions of all the food that will be eaten with asemaa (tobacco) to the side of the portions. The spirit dish is either left outside for the spirits or burned as an offering. I would describe it as kind of like saying grace, a symbol or way of thanking the Creator for the food we were about to eat. This was the way the Ojibwe had always given thanks. Food was a part of every gathering and ceremony.

Larry began the ceremony by removing his ceremonial pipe, which had been holstered in a fringed leather pouch of similar shape. Larry began smoking the pipe while praying in Ojibwe, prayers calling attention to the serious nature of the ceremony.

The Spirit (or Indian) name is given in ceremony

I want to point out that Ma'iingan or Wolf is sacred to the Ojibwe as taught by its Midewiwin spiritual leaders. Next Larry told a story. Every ritual or sacred object is attached to a story.

Gichi-Ma'iingan spoke first in Ojibwe then in English. He spoke in a sacred manner punctuated with touches of humor. He spoke not only of qualities and qualifications of the candidate, and how he came to the name, but reminded all that the naming ceremony has its genesis in - and is part of - the Ojibwe Creation story.

Ma'iingan (Wolf) at that time was in alliance with Original Man, a partnership with humanity, a partnership designed by Gichi-Manidoo Himself.

Original Man along with Ma'iingan were called on by Gichi-Manidoo (the Creator) for the express purpose of naming all things on earth, to go about and give names to all living things. In this journey they became very close to each other. In their closeness they realized they were brothers to all Creation.

They would eventually have to part, but their fates would always be linked.

The Creator said after all was named, "You are now to separate your paths. You must go different ways. But, what shall happen to one of you will happen to the other. Each of you will be feared, respected and misunderstood by the people that will join you on this Earth." So said the Creator.

> *"Rampant and senseless slaughter of bison had the then-desirable effect of greatly reducing both wolves and American Indians. In 1926, the last wild wolf was killed in the US, with the exception of a small population in northern Minnesota. The gray wolf had been "extirpated"—a euphemism for trapped, poisoned, shot, gassed, or any other method of killing you can think of. The general feeling was that the only good wolf was a dead one."* ~Pat Shipman PHD, excerpted from *Who's Afraid of the Big Bad Wolf?* Psychology Today

> *"The only good Indian is a dead Indian."* ~ General Phillip Henry Sheridan

*****

It's real spotty what I remember about the next part of the ceremony, especially the words spoken, as it was more directly related to me. This led me to wonder why I didn't remember. As I thought about it, some of the feelings came back from that day and I remembered something Larry once said about ceremony.

Larry said that ceremony marks a change in life. Moving from child to adult is an easy example. Tribal people, and most of our ancestors, held sacred ceremony when a boy or girl became a man or a woman somewhere around the age of twelve. At the beginning of the ceremony one is a child, and at the end an adult with all the responsibilities and privileges of an adult. That transition period during which the change occurs, is kind of a limbo, neither child nor adult for a time. There is heavy emotion going on so memory fails and/or it's hard to describe.

Larry explained that the one who names has a dream or a vision or a name comes in meditation while thinking about the candidate. Larry said my name came to him while relaxing and looking at the sky right here at the Wellness Lodge, or Obaashiing University.

"And it didn't come easy or right away," said Larry. "So, for a moment I thought to myself, maybe we should name him frog with sunglasses." (I had on shades and I've carried the nickname Makakii or frog for nearly two decades.) Larry often punctuated his teachings with humor.

Larry explained that one is named not for what you've done but for who you are. "Bemidji turned their backs on us, but we also turned our backs on them. Michael acts as a kind of bridge. He built a bridge. Building bridges is not what he does, it is who he is. It is important the work he does to connect the cultures."

I was told that he cited several other complimentary things. Those there present told me that I was crying while Larry was speaking of how he came to the name.

Larry then spoke the name he had given me. He spoke the name Biidaanak-wad, and then translated it to English as Gathering Cloud. I practiced a couple of times how to pronounce the name. Later he wrote it down for me so I have the spelling correct.

Larry's niece Vickie and wife Violet were asked to join me, Vickey to my left, Violet to my right. They each grabbed an arm as if to hold me up. Perhaps they were. First to the east, I said my name "Biidaanakwad," then all in attendance repeated the name in unison, "Biidaanakwad." Violet and Vickie then pointed me to the south, to the west and finally the north, announcing to each of the four directions as was done in the east, "Biidaanakwad."

"One uses their Spirit name when praying," concluded Larry. "When you name something and claim it as yours, then it belongs to you, and it becomes real to you."

The ceremony over, it was time to feast on the foods we brought. A huge crockpot full of wild rice hot dish was nearly eaten. The leftovers we gave to Rose, which seemed to be greatly appreciated. The meal was shared in celebration of the newly named. All lasted about an hour. We headed home about 4:45 p.m.

On the way home, but still on the Reservation, a huge bear ambled across the road west to east. Then, as we passed near the spot we saw the eagle coming up, we saw five eagles looking down upon us, perched in a small clump of bare trees, again from the west.

Coincidences?

Larry once said, "You got to think about what you're thinking about." I found myself thinking about what I thought were interesting occurrences during the 24-hour period starting the evening before and the arrival at home on the day of.

Some seem silly like Barry and Barb…both beginning with BAR (two Bars and a Larry as my we'enh's). Or Larry's wife and sister both answering to names of flowers, Violet and Rose. Another was the two Ikwewag (women) who held me up as I faced the four directions. Both of their names begin with Vi, Violet and Vickey, which seems unlikely to me. How many women's name begin with V at all?

Signs?

The day was Tuesday July 23, 2013. It was the eve of Aabita-niibino-giizis (July or Mid-summer Moon), the day of the full moon. The moon was moving from Capricorn to Aquarius. (My astrologic moon is on the cusp of Capricorn/Aquarius) On this day the Sun moved from Cancer to Leo.

On the way up to Ponemah, Barbara and I saw Migizi (Bald Eagle) and Waagosh (Fox) on the road to Obaashiing just after crossing the line. On the way back to Bemijigamaag we saw Makwa (Bear, Larry's clan) and five Migiziwag (Bald Eagles) high above us in a small forest of bare trees. Barb said there was a Scarlet Tanager among us much of the day too. She said they are often hidden. One animal sighting would be normal for me, but seeing so many critters, and all looking or moving east, seemed unusual.

Biidaanakwad Indizhinikaaz = Gathering Cloud is my name. Aanakwad means cloud, and (the benefactive) biidaw means bring (it) in my dictionary. (Benefaction - an act intending or showing kindness and good will, benevolence, benignity, kindness – a kind act) biidaanakwad vii clouds approach.

I found this amusing as I was going over my notes. At that time I wrote to a friend or two, "I'm going to write about the experience mostly for myself, but will share with family and friends who'd understand. Might take a week."

Perhaps I should have written, "When the time is right, I will write on it." It had been two years.

Part 3

Emails, Quotes and Short Stories

Email Stories, Larry and I

Wolf Event: A Response to the Wolf Hunt

A note from me to Larry, February 03, 2013, I wrote Larry to thank him for speaking at an event that my friend Barry and I put together after Minnesota decided to have a wolf hunt. We brought in both scientific and indigenous views of the wolf.

"My friend, today you were a grand teacher. Many were emotionally moved by your words, even tears. Most agreed that you and the Chairman were the highlights of the program. I greatly appreciate your participation. You helped

me look good.

Weweni, Michael"

Larry responded. "Miigwech. Thank you for making the event possible. You mean something can actually make you look good? :) Thanks again for both you and Barry. Thanks for speaking for Ma'iingan. They know and heard us."

Science

From: Larry to Michael, Friday, April 5, 2013 5:46 PM.

I had written Larry about an article I read with a scientific explanation of "The Truth About Hair and Why Indians Would Keep Their Hair Long." There is a benefit in it. "Science is catching up to some spiritual practices thousands of years old," I wrote, "including American Indian practices of fasting and/or spirit quests. Judeo/Christians have also spoken of the benefits of fasting for thousands of years, as well as Buddhists and others."

Larry answered, "Hey Niiji, should I say wow? Or just be grateful for science? So they are just now beginning to realize or know what we have known since the beginning of creation? Miracles do happen. It may be slow but nonetheless be grateful. What would we ever do without science? :) I guess we can give them credit for the discovery. And just when I always thought this to be common sense, now I read it is science."

Post Naming Ceremony Email July 23, 2013

On August 07, 2013 at 3:26 am, a few weeks after my naming ceremony, I wrote to Larry to tell him I was getting antsy to learn more. I also mentioned attending a Language/Culture Camp for kids.

Larry wrote back a few hours later, "Boozhoo Biidaanakwad, Yeah it's been two weeks since you received and accepted your spirit name, it takes time to get used to and come comfortable with the new state of being, you must use your name in everything you do whenever you are out in nature with all the relatives and relations. It will be good for you to be at the camp to observe and listen. I will be out there too."

Learning from my daughter Kimberly Irene, July 30, 2013

I wrote to Larry that my wife Barb and I had visited our two daughters the previous weekend. While at the home of the elder daughter, she excused herself to attend a fundraiser for a friend suffering from cancer. Absent for several hours, my patience began to be tested. I turned to the TV for distraction.

"I channel surfed and the 3rd or 4th channel I hit I saw your face on the TV," I wrote.. "It was Twin Cities Public TV, and they were showing that program on Ojibwe Language Revitalization. Shortly after you were gone, Tony Treuer started speaking of naming ceremony. My sanity and daughter returned, we had a very good father/daughter chat."

Larry wrote back. "Hey Niiji, so old dogs can still learn new tricks :) So your daughter taught you a lesson. So it's true when the old ones say that the young ones are teachers. It's not so much the teachings but the willingness and openness to learning that counts.

"Oh I'm replacing the lodge, which will probably take me until Friday. There were yellow jackets building a hive on the side of the lodge so I had to get rid of them first before I took the old lodge down. I thanked them for telling me it's time to change the old lodge, but they're still pissed at me for moving them."

Medicine Wheel Colors, March 29, 2014

I wrote Larry looking for Medicine Wheel advice. I had a question about what color represents what direction. "Boozhoo Niiji, We are resurrecting the group Shared Vision. Attached is our logo. I'm thinking that Yellow should be in the East and black in the West making our logo slightly wrong. Am I correct? If it is to be changed, now would be the time. Hope all is well, Chi-Miigwech, Michael"

Larry wrote back, "Boozhoo, good morning. Two things are happening here. Number one, this is someone's vision as it appears. The other is if you're following the Medicine Wheel, then the color yellow is in the east and black to the west. Good idea putting the concept in a circle, that's what gives it life."

The Meaning of "Taking Care of Mother Earth" April 18, 2014

I wrote questioning Larry about his teachings on boundaries, and if I could use the term "personal boundaries" rather than just boundaries in my writing. (When I quoted Larry I wanted to make sure I did not change any meaning.)

"I see the value, the need for, and the symbol of ceremony this evening," I wrote to Larry.

"Hey, I suppose you're sleeping now, this is about the time you sleep isn't it?" Larry said. "You got it, they are personal boundaries. It won't alter the meaning. Well today is Friday, but I can't remember what happens on Fridays. What may I ask do you mean by 'ceremony this evening'?"

"I put the words in the wrong order on ceremony," I answered.

I continued. "Last night I was reading Wikipedia about personal boundaries, and the word 'Liminality' came up. If you don't know, that is the 'time/space that happens during ceremony or is the quality of ambiguity or disorientation that occurs in the middle stage of rituals, when participants no longer hold their pre-ritual status but have not yet begun the transition to the status they will hold when the ritual is complete. During a ritual's liminal stage, participants 'stand at the threshold' between their previous way of structuring their identity, time, or community, and a new way, which the ritual establishes.

"This you know," I went on, "because I hear you speak of ceremony all the time without really explaining its value for healing, as of yet. I remember you saying the old ones are looking for ceremony by the lake. We need ceremony to move through the stages of life, if we do not we might get stuck. Raised a Catholic, I know there is something to ceremony and although they didn't really explain it, there was a feeling of change that I felt.

"I meant last night I had an "aha" moment on ceremony and realized its value to heal. We have lost these things, or many peoples have, as it seems we look toward the Western Judeo/Christian way and have lost that ancient wisdom. During these stages Wikipedia says there is opportunity for the Trickster, but also of growth. I ask myself, when/why did it happen, that all people, who are or were tribal people at one time, throw off thousands of ancient teachings?

"This is what I do at night. Now if I could just figure the connection between your last Power Point title, 'Taking Care of Mother Earth,' and how that fits the teaching on aspects and boundaries. I'm not quite getting the connection yet.

Mii iw minik waa-ikidoyaan, (that's all I have to say) thank goodness eh? Michael"

Larry wrote back. "Hey that's what it's all about. Each one of us was given a path, and as we journey in this physical world, mind you I say physical, today many are lost in a material world which causes the separation. 'Taking care of Mother Earth' comes from the fact we were given the responsibility as care-taker of the earth. Since we are of the earth, to take care of Mother Earth, we do that by taking care of ourselves. It's an interconnected, interdependent and interrelated system. Since we have become separated from the earth we are separated within ourselves too."

Email Stories, Larry Stillday Writes to Barry Babcock

My friend and We'enh (Naming sponsor) Barry Babcock had several email communications with Larry that he shared with me. Barry and wife Linda live off the grid using solar energy for electricity, water from a hand pump, and wood for heat. They live very much off the land. The Babcock's hunt, garden, gather, rice, and sugar bush. They are familiar with local plants and animals for both medicine and food. Barry released his first book this past summer. Published by RiverFeet Press, its title is, "Teachers in the Forest." He quotes and paraphrases Larry's words and teachings particularly where they intersect with environmental science. Many of Larry and Barry's exchanges were about nature.

Medicine of the Wolf

Larry and Barry were having an email conversation about an upcoming visit from Julia Huffman. She was coming to Red Lake for the express purpose of interviewing Larry for her film "The Medicine of the Wolf." Barry, who also would be featured in the film, had arranged the visit.

Larry said in response to Barry sending a photo of Julia; "I'm worrying why she's cussing that guy out. She's pointing two fingers at him not just one. That's got to be serious.

"I'm thinking I need to make a run to the Indian Center in Willmar to get some Indian clothes, You know that's where all the Indians get there Indian clothes now don't you?

"Oh, and I see that the Wolf lady also gave me some titles. I didn't know I was all that."

Nature

When Barry moved "off the grid" to the backwoods of northern Minnesota in June, 2004, Barry shared a story with Larry about a group of ravens that kept flying over at the time, landing in trees…it seemed deliberate, not random, like they were saying hello to new neighbors.

Larry replied; "Yep that's it! So they gave you a welcome when you moved out there. The eagles and the ravens associate with the wolves, it's like they make sure nothing is wasted after a kill.

"When people are balanced and in-harmony with our Earth Mother the animals know that. That's what the old people used to say, 'the animals are talking to us.' Sometimes they use sound, but most of the time they use their behavior. It's therefore up to us to be able to read what they are acting out."

Barry keeps meticulous records on the weather near his area. Barry was telling Larry about his observations of how the animals seem to do so well in spite of the elements.

Larry responded; "Wow what an awakening. You're right. The animals, our relatives, do much better then we human beings who think we know more or better. Our animal relatives simply live with the rhythm of the universe as compared to us who think we can dominate or control the natural laws.

"What we believe is who we are. It doesn't matter what the world says. Our relatives in nature know who we are and that's what matters. All those you mentioned are life, nothing more nothing less, that's equality. It can't get anymore real than that."

Barry wrote Larry about the thanklessness he feels at times when advocating for the environment.

"Hey, Larry," Barry said, "My pump went out on my well and I got roped into attending several public meetings about the latest Enbridge pipeline coming through Hubbard County. I did not get an award other than a kick in the ass. All I ever got from my environmental advocacy is being the Timex watch of Northern Minnesota, - I 'take a licking but keep on ticking.'

Larry responded; "Hey you know what? There will be those that will care. Quite often we don't see those we have made an impact on as we walk our own walk. There are people out there that notice and want very much to be able to walk the path we walk. Yes, even those that imprison themselves with all the material things, they most of all are the ones that envy those of us that walk the simple path.

"Thank you for being on that path as well, Nelson Mandela is right, **use the heart language when you want to speak.**"

"If you talk to a man in a language he understands, that goes to his head. If you talk to him in his language, that goes to his heart." ~Nelson Mandela

Later Barry wrote Larry to say that things were coming together and he got his pump fixed.

Larry responded; "Hey it's good hearing you got your pump working. Of course as you know, that is one of the elements that we depend on. We need the water it doesn't need us. Just like our Mother the Earth, she doesn't belong to us, we belong to her, and to her we go back. We live in an interconnected and interdependent world. How sadly we forget that, or even more sadly is how we can think we can change that perfect system the Creator put in place, which by the way is very simplistic, he made everything so simple, until he created the human being. That's the reason things start to go out of balance, and now Man puts the blame on our relatives the animals to justify his mistakes."

Barry replied; "You speak the truth, Larry. I agree whole-heartedly with you, but you already know that. I have a hen turkey coming around here everyday. I put out a small pile of sunflower seeds for her. I am undecided as to what to do with her: 1. Quit feeding her. Keep feeding her till she's good and fat - then eat her. 3. Keep feeding her and let her be. I think I have enough venison, partridge, potatoes and rice....so I'll keep feeding her as long as she sticks around and let her be."

Larry answered; "I was going to say if you're in need of food then the turkey is there to fulfill his promise to the Creator to take care of his relative the human. On the other hand if you are in no need, then she's there as a guest, and what do you do for guests?

"Hey, I just had lunch and I took the garbage out and darn never froze. It's 16 below here and the sun is shinning like it doesn't even know its cold. I don't recommend that anyone go outside. I didn't even know it snowed yesterday.

"I learned by going outside to move the car. The guy who plows our road and driveway was here. Now I can get out with the living again. However, I was very content in being snowed in, but it being Monday tomorrow I will need to get out to take Violet to the Chiropractor.

"So you're still debating whether you should eat the turkey huh? Well, I guess that's up to you, but it sounds to me like the turkey will live to see its grandchildren run around in Nature, thanks to you."

Barry wrote back; "We often fail to realize how our actions impact animal and plant communities around us. Cutting a tree or leaving it stand, killing an animal or letting it go…can have ramifications far deeper than we could ever imagine…. and the reverse is also true."

"You just spoke of the interconnected system the Creator so graciously put in place so we can thrive in this world," Larry answered. "Along with this interconnected system He gave us Seven Laws, one of those laws being that of Respect. This respect means we honor our relatives, the four-legged, for taking care of us by giving of themselves and all they ask is that we honor their spirit for giving us their flesh to sustain ourselves.

"This law is still as relevant as it was in the beginning. This respect includes us as human beings. In fact this lesson applies especially to how we treat each other. That constitutes harmony and balance.

"Yes it is true we can and do learn a lot from Nature. She's always teaching us, even when we think there is nothing there but empty space. In truth when it comes to Nature there is never an empty space. The only empty space that exists is in the human mind that thinks it knows a lot."

Hunting

Barry was sharing some experiences he had hunting partridge (ruffed grouse) and hunting deer with a bow during the early fall.

Larry replied; "Good Morning Barry, any luck chasing the partridges? They don't run fast you know. I remember hunting them when I was young. I used to think I was an excellent shot, then my grandpa told me they don't run. Anyway, that was the end of my hunting.

"Hey I remember how good the partridges were, my mother used to fry them. I can still taste them now as I speak.

"Hey that's great that you finally got your deer. But I can't help but think that Waawaashkeshi (white tailed deer) finally felt pity watching you running through the bush for a month and decided, well here then. :)) Just kidding. That's great that it offered to fill your freezer for the winter.

"Thank you for sharing your experience, it goes right in line with the teachings I've been using, it's all about connectedness and relatedness and of course interdependence. Another way of putting this is being in alignment with all that is of nature."

Life

Barry wrote Larry bemoaning again that his work with environment issues sometimes is disheartening.

Larry answered; "Where do you get these messages about yourself? To me everyone is talented, gifted and sacred. Some just find and know that earlier, some later, and some it may take some time. But eventually we all get it and have it, and the good thing about that is it shows up in many different ways. Yes we are all related, we are all of the same breath that created everything.

"That's what we refer to as spirit, everything has spirit and its own form or existence including the woman filmmaker, our brother the wolf, and the maple tree that gives of it self so we can live and enjoy life.

"And yes, we can attribute the mess and/or misery that so many are experiencing in life today to the disconnection from our Earth Mother. Many miss the nourishment as well as the nurturing our Earth Mother has for us.

"It is when man decides to place himself at the center, which is the place of our Creator, that Man therefore shifts the flow of the Spirit. And Man strikes out because of the pain he caused himself. In this way Man has reduced everything in life down to a weed, and therefore has no conscience of the harm he creates, and becomes brother killing brother. He doesn't know where to stop or how to stop."

Later, Barry was sharing with Larry about how his young granddaughter was teaching him things about his computer, and he was amazed.

"Hey, that's right, those young ones know more about this technology because it's their world, their time," Larry answered. "I have been having some problems with my old computer, I think it's trying to tell me it wants to retire, so I am going to retire it. Now I'm trying to get used to my new one, just hooked it up this evening. Right now it's working good. I suppose Michael has been keeping you informed, I have been very busy and I don't see no end yet."

Christmas at Walmart

Larry wrote to Barry; "We had an appointment with the Chiropractor, then on over to Burger King. Now everything was going so good up to there. Then we went to Wal-Mart and that's where it all began, people running over and into you and keeps going. It is a mad house. Now I'm home licking my wounds.

"Michael emailed me and said he's going to the Community Christmas Feast at the Casino. I thought about going but after being ran over continuously I decided to come home where it's safe."

Later Larry elaborates on his Wal-Mart experience.

"I went to Bemidji for last minute things and yes I got pulled into celebrating what everyone calls Christmas. I really don't know what I think or believe about this event called Christmas. I know it makes a person spend money, and lots of it for that matter, but I guess it makes people happy. But I have seen many feel down afterwards and don't know for what reason.

"I don't know if my ancestors understood this concept either. To them every single day was a day of giving and that's the way they lived. Maybe it would have been different if they had a Wal-Mart in their time, who knows.

"Today being at Wal-Mart, I witnessed many buying a bunch of plastic things to bring home and wondered where they're going to put all that plastic after the excitement wears off. I can't help but think that somehow, some day the garbage collectors will pick all the plastic up and take it to the dump. All the people I saw today were so happy to eventually contribute to the dump, if not the dump around their yards. Am I being a scrooge?"

Barry wrote to Larry to wish him safe travels on his upcoming trip to Violet's home in Louisiana. He emphasizes the warmer weather and how it differs from using an outhouse at 37 degrees below zero.

Larry answered; "Yep you have to be tough to be out in an outhouse at 37 below, makes you wonder how many souls are out there as we speak. I remember those times quite well. We used to have to run out there all hours in the night, so we quickly learned to be sure to dump early in the evening and hope it would wait until morning, but it didn't always work.

"I hope you have your potbelly stove burning red hot. I don't know if it's going to warm up anytime soon. You know I came into this world with nothing and I'm going to go out with nothing. That's the way I like it.

"The heck with this packing. I've had enough of the packing when we go some place, its way too much work."

Quotes by Subject

Growth/Healing

"We are intended and created to be human."

"We are not human beings trying to learn to be spiritual, we are spirits trying to learn to be human."

"The Now never asks what's coming next."

"Made as comfortable as possible, humans complicate the simplest things."

"Spirituality is not something separate or apart from ordinary life, it is life."

"Hey that's what it's all about! Each one of us was given a path, and as we journey in this physical world - mind you I say physical - today many are lost in a material world which is the cause of the separation."

"You've got to think about what you are thinking about. And it is simple. The Creator made it simple. There are lessons everywhere if we will but pay attention. We make it complicated. Get out of the way. Let life happen. Sometimes we do not start on time or finish on time because something else happened. Let it happen, do not question it or let it cause you stress."

"Find your gift and use it. We are doing as our ancestors did. The people were asked, and then all came together and pooled their wisdom. We're not

closing. We are just beginning. Thank you for sharing with me."

"It's not about Indians, it's about people. All the life forces must come into alignment. The Prophecies tell us that we are now in the time of a great healing. It says the four Colors of the human family are once again given an opportunity to bring each Color's gifts together and create a mighty nation."

"We are fulfilling a prophecy! One of the old prophecies said young people will be born with old spirits. Young people will be going to the drum and singing the old songs. Young people will go to the elders and start asking, asking for directions. And this is what these young people are doing. I'm very proud of them."

"There are four parts to us, mental, physical, emotional and spiritual. These must be in balance as well. We must have harmony in all four. If we do not, we are not well."

"Where do you get these messages about yourself? To me everyone is talented, gifted and sacred. Some just find and know that earlier, some later and some it may take some time. But eventually we all get it and have it, and the good thing about that is it shows up in many different ways."

"Yes we are all related, we are all of the same breath that created everything. That's what we refer to as spirit. Everything has spirit and its own form or existence, our brother the wolf, the maple tree that gives of itself so we can live and enjoy life."

"You know when you do those things like fasting it's about changing the rules for yourself, those are the only things you change. Don't be so hard on yourself, because that doesn't work."

"You know… we've got to quit telling our people what to do and start telling them who they are."

"Most people don't believe in unconditional love anymore. They say you can't get something good for nothing. Even at church, they pass a collection plate."

On Spirit Quest

"Fasting is about taking control back from the body. The actual fast is sometimes harder when on the vision quest. That's where the true test is. But it's fun too. The best time to do it is in the spring. If you can, do it in the spring, then in early autumn."

"Hey niiji, good to hear from you. You sound like you're way out in the woods, which is not a bad place to be when you're wondering about life in general."

"You know the Creator gave all people the same instructions. That's why he put the four colors of people on the Medicine Wheel, including the gifts he bestowed on each race. So it's no surprise to me that it would have a lot of similarities, the teachings are more about our similarities then our differences."

"You know the weather has a tendency to affect people many different ways. That's because it's a good teacher. We just need to listen to the lessons. In other words, we align ourselves to the lessons. The first lesson the seasons teach us is alignment."

"You ask how to prepare for the journey, getting yourself aligned is where to begin."

"The Elders tell us that we have created so many excuses and placed our blame on external things for a long time, and now we're waiting for life to happen. Like waiting for: the right job, the right partner, or for others to get well.

"The Elders say that this has caused us to miss out on living our true lives.

"The Elders are telling us that we are the one's we've been waiting for."

Teachings

"Everything in life is interconnected, interrelated and interdependent on another. This system cannot be changed. When we have a detachment from the system, what we say and what we do affects that system. The hurt of one is the hurt of all. If we see drunks, we don't walk away, because these are all good people."

"As we learn of these things, people will wake up. We will hear something and we say, 'it seems like I knew that,' that 'aha!' moment. It is something deep inside of us all. When a person realizes that, 'I don't know…what I don't know,' then we can begin! We realize then that, 'now I know…that I don't know'. That's when you become teachable. We are saying in effect, 'I'm open to the message'. Our grandpa and grandma lived like that."

"When we break one heart, we break them all, as they are interconnected. If you don't have balance, you are part of the problem, because it's an interconnected system. Health is more than the absence of disease, it is a state of optimal well-being."

"Honesty in facing a situation is to be brave. Always be honest in word and action. Be honest first with yourself, and you will more easily be able to be honest with others. Do not deceive yourself or others."

"Honesty means being an honorable person free from fraud or deception. Honesty means to refuse to lie, steal or deceive in any way. Honesty to the Elders means being true to yourself. The Elders say; 'Never try to be someone else, live true to your spirit, be honest to yourself, accept who you are and the way the Great Spirit made you.'"

"If you tell someone who they are and they believe you, then they will become that."

"People, culture and language change, but the teachings do not."

"Conflict and struggle always goes to light, it is an evolving system. This is a part of life. It is a friend. Conflict equals fight or flight. When conflict starts, get happy because some change is going to occur, the Elders say."

"I was so afraid of wood-ticks 'til I learned I could outrun them."

"I know not what is, or how others see what I see, I only know the impact of what I see, what I hear and feel has on me, which is convenient because then I can't be wrong. But if I'm wrong about thinking I can't be wrong, well then I'm only bullshitting myself."

Balance

"Unfortunately, most of us are experiencing imbalance in our lives today and may not even know why. It is because we have been and still are being taught to only use two realms of ourselves, the 'mental and physical self.' We have forgotten how to use our 'emotional and spiritual self,' and we end up making decisions and choices based only on what we see, hear, smell and measure."

"How we frame our world is very important because the universe works like a mirror. What we see depends on our frame of reference, which affects what we allow ourselves to see and how we look at things."

"When a situation comes up we are either saying yes or we're saying no. From the yes or no an action occurs. The natural law allows us to experience the consequences of our choices. This is the teaching of the natural law no one escapes."

"The earth and the universe were created for a purpose. All forms of life have a purpose. All purposes are guided by a set of principles, laws and values. The principles, laws and values are hidden in each and every one of us.

"We all have blueprints within us as to why we were born and for what we are meant to become. We need to look within to realize our purpose so we can develop our character to express that purpose. We have within us innate knowledge of our own wellbeing. Everything in life has a purpose."

"The Elders say that we do not have the right to end our life, it is not ours to end, because we are not done with what we came here to do."

Ceremony

"The Creator gave us ceremony to teach us how to be human. Ceremony is about how to be human. Ceremonies help you center, to quiet your mind."

"A healing song for all living things, and all colors of the human race, start in the East clockwise, Ozaawaa (yellow), Miskwaa (red), Makadewaa (black), and Waabishkaa (white)."

"Where do we start? We need to start like a child. Our ancestors knew every part of the development of a child and had rites of passage ceremonies."

"Why? What happened? We don't know. But quit teaching that we have lost something. We haven't lost anything! These are our teachings! These are our ceremonies! We still have these ceremonies."

"The Circle is one of the strongest symbols in nature, and symbolism is a powerful language that we were given to understand and communicate with spiritual concepts and truths. Our Ancestors always engaged in ceremonies as a way of honoring all of life; they thrived on symbolism to help them see the world in terms of circles and cycles. Like them, we too can use the same frame-work of symbolism to incorporate the circular and spiral energies."

Homeless Shelter Ceremony (From my news story at the time)

Stillday burned sage while waiting to speak, and then did a pipe ceremony.

Afterwards he spoke to the group. "We must remember that this can happen to anybody. Many of us are only one pay check away from being homeless." Stillday went on to say that he himself was homeless (lived on the streets) for two years after returning from Viet Nam.

"I am so glad the Tribal Council is doing something in this area. This is all part of the healing, we want to thank the fire, the drum, and all of you". Stillday then called on the drum for healing. He asked for four songs, two for

Ogichidaag and two for Ikwewag.

Environment

'The world may yet realize the ancient American Indian environmental ethic. This is important. It begins with us, and we must share this ethic."

"What do you do if your mate is to give birth? I'd be there to hold her hand, to wipe her brow. This is your Mother. Take care of her."

"The way of the mind that was brought to our land has created great danger to our Earth Mother."

"We are to look deep into nature to have a better understanding of every-thing."

"There are many lessons to be learned from the natural world, that's where the Great Spirit put all the lessons we need to fulfill our earth journey."

"The overall philosophy is to re-connect all people to nature and inevitably to themselves. We know that history is a living part of the present."

"We are doing as our ancestors did. The people were asked, and then all came together and pooled their wisdom."

"Sage is one of the medicines. There are more medicines that we were given, but this smudging is a renewing of the covenant of life. It symbolizes the four elements, sage represents the earth, the shell symbolizes water, the burning of course is fire, and the smoke represents air."

"We were put here with original guidelines to help us live in harmony. Our philosophy is in the belief that the Great Spirit works through nature. The children of the earth, which are the winged, finned, insects, the four legged, are all relatives that have a special knowledge of Mother Nature and the cor-responding four directions. Each creature is a helper to aid us when we seek universal knowledge.

"The Four Sacred Directions with the full power of the earth and the sky and all related life, are regarded as the "Sacred Hoop. It is in the spirit world where we are all connected, in this way we become one with all things."

"A friend asked me how come some maple syrup is darker than other syrup. I said the darker stuff is done at night."

A Prayer:

"Grandfather, look at our brokenness. We know that in all creation only the human family has strayed from your Sacred Ways. We know that we are the ones who are divided; we are the ones who must come back together to walk in the Sacred Way. Grandfather, teach us love, compassion and honor that we may heal the earth and heal ourselves."

Seven Fires

"In the time of the Seventh Fire, new people will emerge. They will retrace their steps to find what was left by the trail. Their steps will take them to the Elders who they will ask to guide them on their journey.

"But many of the Elders have fallen asleep and they will wake up to this new time with nothing to offer. Some will be silent out of fear, while others will be silent because no one is asking anything of them.

"The new people will have to be careful in how they approach the Elders. The task of the new people will not be easy, but if they remain strong in their quest, the Water Drum of the Midewiwin Lodge will sound again. There will be a rebirth of the people and a rekindling of the old ways and the Sacred Fire will be lit again."

"Could it be that the road to technology represents a rush to destruction? The road to spirituality represents the slower path that our traditional people have traveled and we are now seeking again. The Earth is not scorched on this trail and the grasses still grow there."

"If we the People of the Earth could wear the face of brotherhood, we would be able to deliver our society from the road of destruction. We can make the two roads that today represent two clashing world views to come together to form a Mighty Nation. We are the "New People of the Seventh Fire".

Language (Ojibwemowin) Revitalization

"Start to listen to the things of nature. Our language is in nature and consequently is still in us. Listen to what your heart is talking about. I learn by observing. I watch and then I understand me. When you learn this, everything is alive. If nature is alive then our language is alive."

(I asked why some Elders are not getting involved with language revitalization) "Whatever the thing is that will bring them out, hasn't happened yet."

"Language is life. We don't call it the language; we live it. It's a living thing. To lose the language loses how to conduct our ceremonies. It's a different way of looking at the world."

"The Drum has always been a part of the Anishinaabe culture. The people's history can be heard in the songs. Preserving the songs means preserving Anishinaabe lifeway's and worldviews."

Medicine Wheel

"The basis of all our teachings is Bimaadiziwin, the Circle of Life."

"Direction of Healing – individual – family – community then responds – then Nation."

"We move in a circle. We must move about the Medicine Wheel to experience nature, we are related. Nature doesn't need us; we need nature."

"When you start your journey, do it in a circle. This is how we are interconnected. The Creator put everything in a circle for us; we need to walk. Everything is there. Every revolution brings clarity, I learn every time I listen to this. The world repeats."

"Practice Non-interference. I will walk with you. If we miss it, we don't go back, we keep going in the circle and pick it up on the next round. Just keep walking."

"Stand up! Keep walking! Everything we do is within a circle. If you miss it the first time, keep walking. It will come around again."

"Imagine a person who thinks they know it all. Not so, they look at the world only from their place on the Wheel. In order to know and understand, one must go around the Wheel, continually looking at the center, and notice how things look differently depending upon ones place on the Wheel. We must walk the Wheel to see how others see."

"The Medicine Wheel is the symbol we use to express and represent the meaning of life, and meaning provides us with purpose and understanding. The symbol of the circle holds a special place of importance in our belief system. There is no hierarchy in a circle, it's about equality."

"On the other hand, as far as the prophesies go, we are now in the time of great healing, it says the four colors of the human family is once again given an opportunity to bring each color's gift together and create a mighty nation."

Sexual Abuse/Gender Roles

Take Back the Night, Equay Wiigamig

"We are doing violence to ourselves now. They have left us alone. Those who brought the violence to us are living their lives. This is the purpose of our ceremony. We are raising our voice against this violence, this hideous violence and resentment. Rely on tobacco and the drum."

"Violence against women was imported, it is not an Ojibwe tradition. Our tradition was one of respect for women and their sacred role in life giving. Social pressure, tradition, and respect prohibited such behavior. As you walk to the lake remember those who have died before offering your tobacco. Remember your mothers, your daughters, cousins, sisters, aunties, remember."

Healing Ceremony (From my news story at the time)

To close out an event regarding sexual abuse, Spiritual Elder Larry Stillday performed a "Healing Ceremony." Stillday first asked the Drum Young Kingbird to do a Healing Song for victims, and invited all who have been a victim (or know someone who has been) to circle the drum.

"Circle and stand near the drum for your family, friends, and relatives, for those who suffer, who are having a hard time, pray that they will heal, here in this place. To live right, we form a circle and we all become one. When you create that circle you are connecting, connecting to all our relatives around the world. Call on our spirits to protect ourselves."

Stillday then explained the rest of the ceremony. Each participant would fill a small black cloth with asemaa (tobacco), tie it and then all proceed to a "Sacred Fire" kindled behind the Events Center. Stillday suggested all walk up to the fire, say a prayer for themselves or others who may have been victims of sexual violence, then toss the black asemaa bag into the fire. The smoke would carry the prayers to the Creator.

Violence

"Every one of us, during our earth walk, will be affected by violence. The honor of one is the honor of all . . .The pain of one is the pain of all."

Men and Women

"We are a diverse people. All our ceremonies are about man and woman. Where did you come from? The silly answer is from my mother and father. But this is true. Your mother and father are contained in you. You must therefore be balanced with the male and female. If you are not, you will be out of harmony and have stress. If you are a man and not in touch with the female, you cannot treat your woman right. We must balance the feminine with the masculine. If you neglect the feminine you will do the same with your partner. The switch around is also true."

Brother Wolf

"The Wolf represents: Humility, Love, Loyalty, Perseverance, Courage, Stability, Teaching, and Intuition. In the natural world, the wolf expresses humbleness in great clarity. His humbleness comes even though he is powerful both physically and spiritually."

"The sanctity of the wolves is so important to Native Americans, as the earliest stories begin with the "wolf-brother. And in the stories when the man and wolves separated and went their own ways, they were told that when one falls, they would both fall. So we've been given that responsibility as caretakers."

"Most Native Americans are not afraid of wolves and are not worried about overpopulation. There is a system in nature that takes care of population and balances things out; man doesn't have to do it."

"The real reason is fear, what a man fears he kills. Fear makes Ma'iingan (wolf) look bigger. Fear is a liar!"

"When man separates from nature, his heart gets hard. He sees the enemy as a weed. We must approach life in a humble manner. Humility is the teaching of Ma'iingan."

On the Wolf Hunt

"Our conversation started with the delisting. But they had already made their plans. The planning was done long before. We are reacting. Don't give them anything to fight. They are looking for a fight. The simplest thing is the most powerful.

"The enemy is a two-headed snake. One is good and the other evil. When they hear our voices, humility draws attention and curiosity from the good helping it to see the evil, and then evil withers. Don't worry about waking them up, stick to your principles.

"Instead of arguing we use humility. Teach through the teaching of the wolf. Humility is a powerful warrior."

"When you separate yourself from nature your heart gets hard. This is an example of that."

"The creator gave us the wolf as a guardian. Our brother needs us to speak for him. The wolf, our brother, is not a separate entity. The wolf, our brother, is inside of us."

"Everything is of the same earth. We were the last created. We need all that was created before, but they do not need us. There goes a good man, the best compliment. The hatred of the wolf comes more from myth and legend than from reality."

"Our first Grandfather was given the task of naming everything. And he called to the Creator and he asked, 'Why does everything have a partner and I don't?' And the Creator gave him the wolf."

"The Creator told the animals, you know, to take care of their brother, the human being, otherwise the human being would not have survived. The animal people said, 'Yes, we will watch our brother. We will give him our hide, we'll give him our flesh, and we'll give him our bones so that he can live.' So we owe that to the animal people. And today, we're going to pay the animal people, especially the wolf, we are going to pay him back by killing him?"

This is a story I was told by Gichi-Ma'iingan as I remember it.

"Original Man or Anishinaabe (some say Nanabozho) along with Ma'iingan (Wolf) were directed by Gichi-Manidoo (the Creator) to go about and give names to all living things. In this journey they became very close to each other. In their closeness they realized they were brothers to all Creation.

The Creator said after all was named, "You are now to separate your paths. You must go different ways. What shall happen to one of you will happen to the other. Each of you will be feared, respected and misunderstood by the people that will join you on this Earth."

Newspaper Story

"Larry Stillday says the sanctity of the wolves is so important to Native Americans, as the earliest stories begin with the 'wolf-brother.

'And in the stories when the man and wolves separated and went their own ways, they were told that when one falls, they would both fall,' said Stillday, 'and so we've been given that responsibility as caretakers.'

Stillday says most Native Americans are not afraid of wolves and are not worried about overpopulation. 'There is a system in nature that takes care of population and balances things out; man doesn't have to do it,' said Stillday." ~DL On-Line 2/27/13 White Earth prepares for first wolf conference By Paula Quam

Film Trailer: Medicine of the Wolf, a film by Julia Huffman (Transcribed by me)

"Everything in life is somehow or another ends up with the four basic elements. What I'm talking about here is interconnectedness. When we get our minds to understand the interconnectedness, then we are into the interrelatedness. We are related to all things. We are a relative to all things.

"And the Wolf is part of our religion, if we call it a religion. It's part of our lives. If we took the bible and put legs on it, and somehow mechanically do that, and send it into the woods, and it's able to walk around the woods, and we get our guns and start shooting the bible, they'd put us in jail because we're desecrating their religion."

Short Stories

Red Lake Tragedy, Interview with Gichi-Ma'iingan

By Dan Gunderson, Minnesota Public Radio, March 25, 2005

Original Lead "Tribal elder's protective of Red Lake culture"

Ojibwe involved in the Ponemah services declined to describe details. Tribal elder Larry Stillday said the practices could only be appreciated by seeing them.

"The depth of it is way beyond a conversation with somebody," he said.

Ponemah, Minn. — Ponemah is a place where most people still speak the Ojibwe language. They practice the same ceremonies their ancestors practiced long before Europeans arrived in North America.

Larry Stillday prefers to be known by his Indian name, Gichi-Ma'iingan. He says traditional ceremonies can't be easily understood. Ceremonies are not a prescribed static event, but a living, breathing extension of the people who are participating.

"My experience is people come to us and talk about our culture, and say, 'OK, now we understand it.' And they miss the whole depth of it," says Gichi-Ma'iingan, "because our ceremony and our language is all of who we are, the earth, the sky, everything. So the depth is way beyond just having a conversation with somebody.

So what happens is, it's left to the outside world the interpretation of who we are."

Gichi-Ma'iingan says the interpretation of Indian ceremonies is too often a one-dimensional representation, and only captures a moment in time when tragedy grabs the attention of the outside world. The focus is on what's visible, the ceremony. The deeper spiritual meaning is missed.

"It is not that we don't want to share, but they approach us as teachers in the same sense as standing in front of the classroom and teaching. It is not that way," says Gichi-Ma'iingan.

He says traditional beliefs and ceremonies can only be understood when they've been experienced. That's why recording and photos are not allowed at many of the most sacred ceremonies. The elders believe this would encourage superficial understanding of their culture.

Gichi-Ma'iingan has strong distrust of people who suddenly express deep interest in his beliefs when there is a tragedy.

"When I get up and go outside my house and get ready to go to work, no cameras, no tape recorders, so I'm an invisible human being. But we here on the reservation do our work like anywhere else," says Gichi-Ma'iingan. "And when a tragedy happens, all of a sudden here they are. 'I have a lot of questions for you.' My advice is, come over to my house and visit when there is no tragedy. And then I can talk with you."

*****

"Ojibwes involved in the Ponemah services declined to describe details. Tribal elder Larry Stillday said the traditions practiced by the tribe can only be appreciated by seeing them — not by talking about it.

'The depth of it is way beyond a conversation with somebody,' he said." ~NBC News, 3/26/05

First Speakers, Round House, 2010

KTCA hour long production "First Speakers: Restoring the Ojibwe Language." This is just a three and a half minute excerpt about the Ponemah Round House. My transcript follows.

Larry "Well right now we're heading out to the Round House, and the Round House is one of the things the elders requested that it be constructed because that is one of the ceremonial lodges that our ancestors used to have."

- Break- Comments by Anton Treuer

Larry "The doors are placed in the direction of east/west and that is significant to us for the ceremonies. The east door is where all things begin the new day, and basically the west door we're facing the west at the end, it's the direction where all things end.

"You know one of the first designs that was created, was a circle. And everything after that was placed inside the circle. And therefore everything moves in a circle. Even the human from childhood to childhood, the seasons go in a circle. All the stars, the sun and moon, the earth, they always move in a circle. And what that creates is what they call a rhythm, there's a universal rhythm. Every time we do a ceremony we align all these things. You see we call these things, all the principles and values to be in alignment. Back in the days when they were used, that was part of what we now call language, that was just basically a day of living."

Alignment

Excerpt from a story by Molly Miron, The Bemidji Pioneer, July 7, 2012 regarding Red Lake July 6 Independence Day Powwow

"Following the Grand Entry Friday, Spiritual Leader Larry Stillday opened the main events with a prayer. He explained that the traditions are not just Anishinaabe or Spiritual, but for everyone. 'It's really about being a human being,' he said, 'It's about being here on the earth.' He said his opening remarks (in Ojibwe), 'call the powers into alignment. It gets everybody into the natural rhythm of the universe.'"

Appeasement Ceremonies at Several Red Lake Sites, August 2012

"One severs the connection of earth and water by connecting them." ~Gichi-Ma'iingan

I asked Stillday if I should try to explain the symbolism behind the story I wrote below for the Red Lake newspaper and Red Lake Net News. He said he wouldn't bother as it would not be understood by most, and those that would understand, already knew. Nonetheless….

On Friday, August 17, 2012, from 1 to 4 pm, the Red Lake DNR Water Resources Program invited tribal members to participate in Appeasement Ceremonies for Lake Access Stabilization and Mud River Stream Restoration Projects.

The appeasement rituals were officiated by Spiritual Leader, Larry Stillday. The ceremonies were held because of recent lake access stabilization, erosion control, and stream restoration work. Two vans were made available for those who wanted to car pool.

Those participating moved from east to west, according to custom, starting at the Blackduck River Lake access, then to the "cut-off," then proceeded to the Fisheries, Mud River, McKenzie, and concluded at Hallet Landing near Little Rock.

Lake access work involves storm water control and stabilization of the access roads and boat ramps to reduce the amount of run-off entering Lower Red Lake. Exposed soil and erosion of lake access roads and ramps contribute to phosphorus and sediment loading of Red Lake. Stabilizing these lake accesses promotes better water quality, and provide clean habitat for fish in Red Lake.

Appeasement then is a response to scarring the land and the Sacred Lake. This is a symbolic act to let the spirits of the earth and water that we are penitent for that transgression. The land had been disturbed where ancestors lived and where some may even have been buried. There is a need to ask for forgiveness for disturbing these site types as well. Shards were found at some sites and sent to the University of Minnesota and were found to be 2000 years old, long before the Dakota or Ojibwe occupied this area.

Spiritual leader Larry Stillday was appeasing ancestral spirits because of the disturbances to the earth and water, two of the four elements. "We are asking for forgiveness, we are giving an apology or appeasement for the disturbances."

Blackduck River Lake Access and Fisheries Site

The reason the Fisheries was included in the appeasement ceremonies was because of a cement slab put into the lake back in the 30's. Something similar happened at the site at Blackduck River.

Docks and slabs are artificial or man-made things. Things that belong to the water belong to the water and earth things to the earth. Cement and bituminous slabs into the lake are not part of the water but part of the land or the earth. At Blackduck the slab will be taken from the lake and be replaced by blacktop but only to the edge, not into the water.

The McKenzie Site

At the McKenzie site, there was a burial mound. Eight years ago it was dug into (without knowledge of its importance) during grading. Being close to the lake, the mound started eroding into the lake. As a result, human remains were found. Police took the remains suspecting it to be a homicide, but found that the remains were much older. Some then wanted to carbon date the remains, but Spiritual Leader Waasibiik (Anna Gibbs) was against it. Gibbs took charge and reburied the remains in an unknown place.

The erosion still occurring, Stillday had instructed the DNR to reinforce the mound, but not to mark it for fear of curiosity seekers.

Hallet Landing

The site at Hallet Landing was the final ceremony of the day. When the access was built at Hallet, pottery shards were found during the ground disturbance. "There may have been something here related to settlement," said Jenilynn Bohm, Red Lake DNR Non-point Source Pollution Specialist at the time. "Some shards found were 2000 years old."

At Hallet Landing, the disturbance included a road as well as the landing. "Our ancestors of course built their communities near water for all that it offered including transportation," noted Stillday. "There could be burials near the water because dams have made the lake larger expanding the shoreline, so graves that appear to be near or on the shore probably were not in times gone by, (because of erosion possibilities) although then as now they would be near communities."

The ceremony conducted by Stillday included the planting of an oak post off to the side of the landing, just a bit out of site and to the East, symbolized (or is) a "medicine tree." The purpose is to create energy according to Stillday. About eight inches at the top of the post was debarked and painted red. After the planting, a red ribbon was tied to the post where the paint met the bark. The red paint where the ribbon was tied is called the "bloodline." A tobacco pouch was attached to the ribbon as an appeasement offering. The bloodline symbolizes the re-connect or appeasing of the ancestral spirits as well as the earth (land) and water.

After further prayer now at the lake, a birch-bark spirit dish (containing food) was placed in the water hidden behind a most convenient rock. According to Gichi-Ma'iingan, this symbolized the interconnectedness of earth and water and all the elements, as well as people, plants, and all living things.

"Gaabeshiwin" (The Camp), Ponemah Round House, Summer, 2013 (Excerpted from the story I wrote at the time)

"The overall philosophy is to re-connect all people to nature and inevitably to themselves. We know that history is a living part of the present."

Order of Creation

In the group conducted by Spiritual Advisor and First Speaker Larry Stillday, the elder spoke of Gimishoomisinaan Giizis, (Grandfather Sun) Noosinaan Giizhig, (Father Sky) Gookomisinaan Dibiki-giizis, (Grandmother Moon) and Gimaamaanaan Aki. (Mother Earth)

Stillday spoke of the Order of Creation and how it relates to the Medicine Wheel. "First came minerals. Next came plants, animals were the third order of creation, and humans were created fourth and last," said Stillday. "Those created next are dependent upon those created before it. Minerals are fine on their own, while humans, created last, depend on all that came before. We are of the earth, we are these elements, and the trees clean the air so we can breathe. We need to take care of them."

Little Rock Language Revitalization Powwow:

A community powwow, an extension of the camp, was held the second night. An elder woman dropped an eagle feather fan. This is serious. I have heard it described as "eagle feather down" and everything stops. Reconciliation must happen. A Mide or other accepted person must pick it up and perform a short ceremony before giving it back to the person who dropped it. Larry picked up the fan and while he said prayers in Ojibwe facing each of the four directions, the woman walked around the circle alternating between English and Ojibwe kind of letting it all out about how she felt about "Manifest Destiny."

I wrote at the time:

Drum songs preceded words offered by elders and first speakers. Shortly thereafter, an eagle feather fell upon the ground. Youth and others, some perhaps for the first time, had the opportunity to witness the sacred manner in which such things are handled.

After praying to the four directions in Ojibwe and returning the fan to the woman, Gichi-Ma'iingan said, "Everything is a circle. Take a look about you, the first circle is the drum, then we form a larger circle around them, and so on until we encompass the entire earth."

"Earth Mother, Father Sky, all our relatives, we ask our grandfather, to bring all peoples together. We have enough people who look backward — those who remember — this is good, but we need more to look forward. We need to lead the way, our culture, our arts and crafts, we are alive TODAY!"

Closing Words from Gichi-Ma'iingan at the First Gaabeshiwin, 2013

At the close of this three-day culture camp, all ended with a drum song, and words of wisdom from some of the elders, notably Eugene Stillday who told several humorous stories and Larry Stillday who ended on a more serious note.

There were 50 rambunctious kids, 6 to 13 years old on a warm summer day. Larry started talking and much to my surprise, the youngsters quieted.

"I've seen a lot of wisdom here. The kids picked up on what was going on right away and took a chance to express themselves," said Gichi-Ma'iingan. "I taught no one, they taught me, they taught me what I don't know."

"Nothing is lost," Stillday went on. "Let the little ones live. No one is coming from across the sea to hurt them. They are going to sing the words of the old people. This has been a powerful healing. Wisdom is here. Each child has a gift. We provided an opportunity. I don't want these kids to believe they have lost something.

"Yes, they are speaking our language. It is like singing, singing a song that the old ones want to hear. The young ones will never know there was a loss. We provided a place for them. This is where they are from. Quit teaching that they have lost something. Our youth will pick it up. We just have to give them the opportunity. This has been nothing but learning. All will go away with something. All will go away as better people."

Sobriety Run, 2013 (From the Story I wrote at the time)

"The run is of historical, cultural and spiritual significance," said Red Lake Spiritual Elder Larry Stillday.

"I've been out there doing invocations for the runners," said Stillday. The run is a prayer. The first day is run for those suffering, the second day is run for gratefulness for positive things.

"A message is carried for all families. The run has adopted this principle, it's more than about alcohol and drugs, it's about wellness and health in the broadest sense. When the run sends its energy into the inter-connective web, it is spiritually significant, we are dealing with the web of life. People who are in the city will feel it…they will feel it, and in the same manner you will feel humility. This is the teaching; Elders say the spirit is constantly in motion. The person running activates emotion, which goes into the rhythm of life. That's how connected we are, connected to all people, and all living things."

Talk Before Calvary Lutheran Church,

as told by Leo Soukup

It was in early 2014 at Calvary Lutheran Church in Bemidji. About 40 people met between services. Leo had invited Larry. At one point Larry drew a stick figure with a huge head, and said, "This was me. I just thought about things. Then I learned there were other parts to take care of."

"Where does Jesus fit into this," asked one member? According to Leo it was a gotcha question, implying paganism, or some such thing.

Larry was cool as a cucumber according to Leo. Larry said, "Well Jesus walked the earth and he told stories, parables, walked among the people, helping people. And that's what we do. We go visit people, help those with little money, visit the sick and we tell stories as a way to teach."

*****

"I will be doing a presentation on death and dying in Rochester Mayo Clinic. I'm getting ready to go speak with some students from Cretin Durham High School in St. Paul. They come up here every year, then they will go away having learned something about life or even more confused than before," Larry said with a smile.

Outtake: Interview for the Film Medicine of the Wolf

Courtesy Julia Huffman Director Medicine of the Wolf

Interviewer: How does the wolf help us with our purpose?

Larry: Our relationship with the wolf goes a long way back in history. It goes a long way back. The relationship goes way back to the beginning of time. The wolf has always been with us, and the reason that our brother the wolf has been with us since the beginning of time, is because in terms of creation story, our first grandfather was given the task of naming everything in creation.

And as he began his journey, he began to realize that everything in creation came in twos. They had partners. And the man asked the Creator, "Why does everything have a partner and I don't?"

So the Creator spoke to him and said, "I give wolf to accompany you on your journey, on your task. So that was the beginning of our relationship with the wolf. He walked with our first grandfather as he walked over the whole world naming everything.

So the wolf has a really big role. He is a very significant part of who we are. There is no separation between the wolf and us. I'm not talking about a physical separation, I'm talking about a spiritual connection, and that is unfortunately something that man today does not see. The man lost sight of that spiritual connection with a lot of things, and this is the reason that he puts himself above.

Because of his lack of that connection…when you have emptiness…you may have the absence of that connection, you're going to have to do something, and one of the most obvious things to do is to put yourself above everything else.

Interviewer: Fear?

Larry: And see that's when it began to shift. And at the time that our first godfather completed his task, the Creator spoke to him and said; "Now you will go your separate ways, but the parallel fate of your lives will be the same. Whatever happens to the wolf will happen to you. What happens to you will happen to the wolf." So the connection still remains even if they are not physically connected.

And so what we're talking about when we have a connection, we're not talking about a physical connection, although it is part of the spiritual connection. And the spirit of the wolf knows that, you know, the spirit of the Anishinaabe knows the connection. And that is what the world does not see today because in the world advertising is everything. And when you advertise something it's going to be lessening.

Interviewer: Do you think we want to own it because of the lack we have in ourselves?

Larry: When you have that void inside you're going to try to fill it with something. See, and what are you trying to fill it with? And I tell you, whatever it is that's out there, you want to possess that. What that means is that they try to reach outside themselves to fill that void. When the fact is that you can fill it from within.

And that's that spiritual connection that we have as a people to all things in nature. We still have that. Although because of what happened to us, you know…in our history…we experience the void. And when we experience the void we start reaching out to the physical. And one of the first things was alcohol. So we grabbed that.

And sadly there was a time; there was a place in which we began to ceremonialize liquor.

Interviewer: Worship it?

Larry: To justify the fact that we used liquor we ceremonialized it. Ceremonializing, that just means that we then become higher than the plant, the spirit of the woods. We placed ourselves above.

Interviewer: It seems like we're always searching for God.

Larry: People ask me, just last weekend I was able to do a speech and, and I checked, you know, and there was an older guy there, there was a lot of old people and the first thing I said, "Oh, no." And so I started and they were listening, and one guy said; "Yeah, but where does the Father, the Son and the Holy Spirit fit in here? I don't see it."

And I did sort of turn the light off and flip charts, you know. He said, "Do your people believe in the Father, the Son and the Holy Spirit?" I said, "Yeah." He said, "Well I don't see it." I walked over and said, "Here, He is right here. Because everything in creation is about God, God is right here in everything. That is God. And if you want that he had a son."

"Yeah," he said, "yeah, but where's the Son?"

"Right here," I said. "A human being has emotional, spiritual, physical and mental aspects, and he's also got five senses. Is that the Son? Did the Son come to me in the physical world? That's Him right there."

Oh, oh. Nobody ever explained that to him. Nobody ever told him. He hadn't thought of it that way. Even though they know Jesus became a human being. To me it is emotional, spiritual, to experience that. And so he just sort of backed off, you know, I mean he just kind of stared at me, and basically it's all right there and some can't even see it.

Interviewer: Thinking about the wolf and the relationship the Ojibwe had to wolf, did you make a declaration about the outside coming to the reservation to hunt?

Larry: But you know, when you're talking about the hunting or non-hunting side of the reservation no, we didn't put it there. You see that's nothing, we didn't put it there. We didn't say you couldn't hunt here. If we made the reservation, then we can say you can't hunt here. So who put us on the reservation?

And then they looked at us and said that the Injuns were saying you can't. I said wait a minute. You know, the government made the reservations, we didn't. We're just saying this is, this is where we live. You know, and you can't come where we live.

Interviewer: It's just about living the way you live.

Larry: The government is the one that put the reservation lines.

Interviewer: You showed me the lines.

Larry: And the people that come and say you can't hunt on the Indian reservation, go talk to your government. They're the ones that made the reservations. We didn't.

Interviewer: Right. It's just a matter of being who you are.

Larry: Still, I mean to really think about it. Who made the reservations? But it's just a way for people will to say, "Well the Indians say that we can't." The Indians had no say when they were put on the reservation. And then the Indians accepted the fact that there's a reservation, "Oh we've got a line. And that line is ours." And that's what they're saying. They didn't say we put that there.

The government put us inside this line. And that's something people don't think about. People they don't, and that is because they are disconnected. There's an old spiritual saying that says when a man moves away from nature his heart becomes hard. And that is so true. That is so true, and that's what we're dealing with today.

Interviewer: Do you see a reflection of the violence that's going on out in the world as related to the violence that's going on directed at nature?

Larry: Actually from nature! We are disconnected from nature. In the beginning the earth was created and on the earth was put everything that the human being was ever going to need to make its' walk. When we see some change among the earth, that's when man disconnected it. Where man removed himself from it…not removed him…put him in the center.

Interviewer: So we don't see wolves or wildlife as being feeling, connected to God, an important part of the eco-system?

Larry: What happens benefits the whole. They establish a hierarchy, you know, who's going to be the dominant. Not because they just want to be the rulers, no they're thinking of the whole pack. In unity there's strength in the pack. They hunt together.

And they use the word killing. They use the word killing. Wolves don't kill. They eat. Because that's the way they're programmed. They are programed to eat and to support their families. Just like anything else. They're supporting. Now we go into their territory and bring domestic animals in there. They don't know how to do anything but be domestic. (LAUGHS) And it so happens to be in the back yard of a wolf family. And then they blame the wolf for being there.

Interviewer: We're in their home.

Larry: And we don't take account, we don't admit…it's ok, I moved there. No, they say the wolves came to where I moved. That kind of thinking, there's something wrong with the thinking here, huh?

And as far as our relationship with the wolf, we are talking about the ceremonial lodge here. This is a ceremonial building, these roundhouses and stuff like that. It's something basic, the structures that they used back then.

But all included the animals. They included all of the animals. They included the four legged, they included the swimmers, they included the winged ones and they also included the crawlers. They included those in the ceremony. And so when you're thinking badly of the wolf, the bear, they're included. See?

And the reason that they're included in there is because in the old times, at the time of the creation the Creator told the animals to take care of their brother the human being. Otherwise the human being would not have survived. The animals said, "yes, we will watch over our brother."

We will give him our hide. We will give him our flesh. We will give him our bones so that he can live. So we owe that to the animal people. And today we're going to pay the animal people and especially the wolf. We're going to pay them back by killing them. You know we need to seriously think about thinking.

Interviewer: We've been taking a lot as a society.

Larry: You know you ever seen these hunters go out there? There was one day I was walking along and boom, I bumped into something and said, "Oh man, what was that?" And there was a guy standing there, he was dressed in camouflage. I couldn't see him. And he even had a hat backwards. The visor was in the back. I think before we had the caps in the front for some reason. Didn't they?

You know, ever since I seen them I've been going to stores everywhere I go. I stop and I'm looking for a cap. They said, "Can I help you?"

So I said, "Yes I'm looking for a cap." And they said, "Well here's our caps." I said, "No, not those." I said, "I'm looking for the one with the visor in the back." (LAUGHS) One girl said, "No sir, you just turn it around."

Interviewer: It's a strange style.

Medicine of the Wolf: Behind the Scenes:

Courtesy Julia Huffman Director Medicine of the Wolf

Transcription of Transcription by Michael Meuers

An Outtake video 17 minutes long. At 5:04 we see and hear Gichi-Ma'iin-gan (Larry Stillday) speak of smudging. This is followed by Larry telling a bit about the Ojibwe Creation Story and the roll that Ma'iingan (Wolf) plays in the Ojibwe World View (Spirituality). Ends 8:16.

Smudging

Larry: "And so people ask, what is this ceremony? This is a smudging ceremony. Yes, it is. And what does it do? Well, you know it purifies. It purifies. Some people say, 'Well it takes away negative energy.' You know they have all these explanations and such. Okay good, but that's actually (only) the ceremony itself. But what they miss is the fact that this is basically about respect. Respect, because you're using the four basic elements here.

"Everything we do in the ceremony always goes back to the four basic elements. There's fire, water, earth, and air. (Holding up smudge bowl) There's fire, water, earth and air in this. Everything in life, somehow or another, ends up with the four basic elements. It always consists of the four basic elements."

Interviewer: "How does the Wolf teach us our purpose, or help us with our purpose?"

Larry: "It goes a long ways back. In terms of creation story - who we call our first grandfather - was given the task of naming everything in creation. And as he began his journey, he began to realize that everything in creation came in twos. They had partners. And he approached…he called on the Creator and says, 'Why does everything have a partner and I don't?' So the Creator spoke to him and says, 'Ma'iingan (Wolf) will accompany you. He will accompany you on your journey, your task.'

"So that's part of the beginning of our relationship with the wolf. There is no separation between the Wolf and us. I'm not talking about a physical separation. I'm talking about a spiritual connection. And that's a connection that man today does not see. The man lost sight of that spiritual connection to all things. And this is where, why the reason that he puts himself above. Because he's lacking that connection."

Bemidji United Methodist Church Bulletin, Mother's Day 2014

"On Mother's Day, Elder Larry Stillday will be our guest speaker in worship!

Mr. Stillday is an elder, spiritual advisor, teacher, and community leader from Red Lake. He and his wife, Violet, graciously accepted an invitation to speak to us about our relationship with the earth and the spiritual connections at the heart of stewardship of creation.

"As United Methodists committed to "faith that seeks understanding," we welcome the Stillday's and the earth wisdom of our Ojibwe brothers and sisters. Come and celebrate God's good gifts of mothers and our planet!"

From "Blood Struggle: The Rise of

Modern Indian Nations"

Chapter: "Indian Country: August 1953" by Charles F. Wilkenson 2005 "No Sense of Entitlement" Larry Stillday, interview with author, Red Lake reservation, Minnesota, March 23, 2001

"Larry Stillday, a little boy in the 1950's grew up in Ponemah, the most traditional village on the Red Lake Reservation. The people there still bury their dead in the earth under spirit houses, wooden structures the size of a grave with pitched roofs and sides just a foot or two high. Slender and graceful, Stillday talked in his soothing voice about the reservation of his childhood. 'We had no sense of entitlement. We had the loss of land. We had the loss of religion to the missionaries. The religion was taken. The absence of children was quite noticeable. Our children were being ripped away, to government boarding schools, to non-Indian foster homes off the reservation. Losing children is like losing the land.

'You talk about losing the land, and you talk about acreage, but that is not the whole part. There is the sacredness. During the Korean conflict there were bombings (when the military conducted practice maneuvers). As a child I'd be swimming in the lake. Jets would come over and drop bombs back in the woods. Boom. Boom. They never had permission to do that. Another intrusion was through logging after the war. It was another form of attack.'

As a young man Stillday left the reservation for Minneapolis, and he lived for a while in Europe, staying away for thirty-five years. Now he is a counselor for the tribe in Ponemah. 'It was a confusing time, a time of hopelessness. We were aware of all these things, assimilation, and acculturation. Kids today have the choice to come back. They know they have an entitlement. They know they are entitled. We didn't have that choice.'"

From the Book: "God Grant Me: More Daily Meditations from the Authors of Keep It Simple" From the page for February 17.

"The Now never asks what's coming next." ~ Larry Stillday.

"We need to spend some time every day in the Now. Just being. Just being enough. Relaxing. Enjoying the people around us, or enjoying a moment alone. Listening to our heartbeat. Feeling the air enter and leave our bodies as we breathe calmly and deeply. Trusting that, for this moment, all is at it should be. Life is taking care of us. We are in our Higher Power's care.

In this moment, we let go of the past and we let go of the future. We focus on Now. Now we don't think. We simply listen. To our heartbeat. To our breathing. To the sounds of life around us. To the quiet voice of our Higher Power."

Medicine Wheel Primer

The Ojibwe Medicine Wheel

Traditional teachings of the Ojibwe people encompass all aspects of the person's life in relation to the world around them. The learning process addresses and teaches about the inseparability of the emotional, physical, intellectual and spiritual dimensions. Ojibwe people believe that everything happens goes in a circle clockwise, therefore the Medicine Wheel is a circle divided into four quadrants.

The Medicine Wheel is an interconnected system of teachings relating to the seasons, directions, elements, colors, and the cycle of life. It speaks of the need for balance, harmony and respect as bringers of happiness. It is an ancient system of traditional indigenous knowledge that many tribal peoples share under many different names. Experience continues to be a fundamental principle of the Anishinaabe learning process.

There are two aspects: the Seen world made up of physical and mental, and the Unseen world made up of emotional and spiritual. It is about ceremony. All that is life is in the Medicine Wheel. It is full of symbols and teachings.

Seven Sacred Teachings Primer

"Made as comfortable as possible, humans complicate the simplest thing."
~Gichi-Ma'iingan

The Gifts

Wisdom • Love • Respect • Bravery • Honesty • Humility • Truth

To cherish knowledge is to know **Wisdom**

To know **Love** is to know peace

To honor all of creation is to have **Respect**

Bravery/Courage is to face the foe with integrity; (being complete or undivided)

Honesty in facing a situation is to be brave

Humility is to know yourself as a sacred part of creation

Truth is to know all of these things

Regarding Honesty vs. Truth

Honesty is subjective; Truth is objective. Honesty is your interpretation of the truth, but that interpretation may be incorrect. You may honestly believe that the world is flat, but it in fact, in truth, it is round.

The Seven Sacred Teachings or Seven Laws or

How to be human

Background

Among the Anishinaabe people, the Teachings of the Seven Grandfathers, also known simply as either the Seven Gifts or Seven Grandfathers', is a set of teachings on human conduct towards others.

According to the *Aadizookaanaan* (traditional stories), the Teachings were given to the Anishinaabeg early in their history. Seven Grandfathers asked their messenger to take a survey of the human condition. At that time the human condition was not very good. Eventually in his quest, the messenger came across a child. After receiving approval from the Seven Grandfathers, tutored the child in the "Good way of Life." Before departing from the Seven Grandfathers, each of the Grandfathers instructed the child with a principle.

Red Lake Healer and Elder, Gichi-Ma'iingan teaches that, "There are many lessons to learn from the natural world, that's where the Great Spirit put all the lessons we need to fulfill our earth journey. We are to look deep into nature to have a better understanding of everything."

The Teachings of the Seven Grandfathers

and the Animal Guides

As Taught to me by Gichi-Ma'iingan, Larry Stillday

There are many field guides and other writings available for us to examine the natural science of wildlife, which reside along the North Country Trail in Minnesota. But infrequently do we have the opportunity to see wildlife as the traditional Ojibwe have for untold centuries.

There are many lessons to be learned from the natural world, that's where the Great Spirit put all the lessons we need to fulfill our earth journey. We are to look deep into nature to have a better understanding of everything.

The Elders tell us that connecting with animal guides helps us to be a better person. We will be healthier, physically, mentally, emotionally and spiritually. We will see the world and all things in it with clarity and understanding.

We can learn a lot from animals, both from the physical and spiritual form by watching the animals around us. We learn how to live with nature and trust our instincts. Our animal spirit guides can bring us messages of guidance and offer protection to shield us from negative energies. But we must be open to our animal spirits and the messages they bring.

Every animal is different just like we are, each having their own attributes that gives them advantages in their day-to-day life. Every experience we have with animals has something to teach us. We may have a connection or attraction with a certain animal.

We were given the Teachings of the Seven Grandfathers to act as our spiritual foundation. These laws offer direction for anyone who wishes to have a balanced life. An animal represents each teaching or law. The teachings of the animal world offer us the help we need to live close to the natural laws.

Amik (Beaver) represents Nibwaakaawin (Wisdom)

To cherish knowledge is to know Wisdom. Wisdom is given by the Creator to be used for the good of the people.

To know and understand Wisdom is to know that the Great Spirit gave everyone special gifts to be used to build a peaceful and healthy community. Amik uses his sharp teeth for cutting trees and branches, a special gift he received from the Great Spirit. The Beaver represents; Determination, Strong Will, Gatherer, and Accomplishment.

Migizi (Bald Eagle) represents Zaagi'idiwin (Love)

Migizi in Anishinaabe creation stories was a savior for man by showing his Love for them before the Great Spirit. Symbolically, Migizi is the one animal that can reach the highest in bringing vision to the seeker. Migizi values are divine spirit, clear vision, great healing powers, courage, sacrifice, and connection to the Creator.

To feel Love is to know the Great Spirit, therefore, it is expected that our first Love is to be the Great Spirit. Love given to the Great Spirit is expressed by loving oneself, if we can't love ourselves; it is impossible to love anyone else. The Eagle was chosen by the Great Spirit to represent this law.

Mashkode-Bizhiki, (Buffalo or Bison) represents Minwaadendamowin (Respect)

Every part of the Buffalo provided Native People's with some valuable tools for life; shelter, clothing, food, utensils, and even fuel for fire – its dung for daily living. Through giving its' life and sharing every part of its' being, shows the deep Respect it has for people. Bizhiki teaches us that Respect must be given toward all life, and understand the interconnectedness of all life.

The attributes of the Buffalo are; Life, Sacredness, Healing Powers, Abundance, Stamina, Provider, and Sacrifice. Once we understand our interconnectedness, we will get very clear understanding of our dependence on the land; therefore give the land and its resources absolute Respect.

Makwa (Black Bear) represents Aakwade'ewin (Courage or Bravery)

In its natural home, Makwa shows us the spirit of Courage. To have Courage is to overcome our fears that prevent us from living out our true spirit as human beings.

To have Courage is to have the mental and moral strength to listen to our heart.

By nature Makwa is a very gentle creature, but threaten its cub and it will display total fearlessness in defending her cub. The virtues taught us by Makwa are power, industriousness, instinctive healing, gentle strength, introspection, dreams, and living of the heart-living spirit.

The Bear is very close to the land and brings many medicines to our people. Because of his claws, which are good for digging, Makwa pays attention to healing herbs that many other animals pass up. Makwa is closely connected to the Midewiwin (Grand Medicine Society) as a teacher. Midewiwin members are said to "follow the Bear path."

When we have a hard time in our life, whether it is something we are going through or a decision we have to make, and we are afraid, we can call on the spirit of Makwa to help us have the Courage and strengths to do the right thing for our life. Makwa is the part of the self that needs to retreat into its own space, hibernate and heal itself. It is comforting and protective, and a common animal spirit for mothers.

Misaabe (Giant, Wilderness Man or Bigfoot) represents Gwekowaadiziiwin (Honesty)

Misaabe represents the essence of Honesty and innocence. Honesty means being an honorable person free from fraud or deceptions. Honesty means to refuse to lie, steal or deceive in any way.

The Elders say; "Never try to be someone else: live true to your spirit, be honest to yourself, accept who you are and the way the Great Spirit made you." They say the highest honor that could be bestowed upon anyone is the saying, "There walks an honest person, he can be trusted." Then and only then might you accept others for who they are. Honesty to the Elders means being true to yourself.

Ma'iingan (Wolf) represents Dibaadendiziwin (Humility)

Ma'iingan represents: loyalty, perseverance, courage, stability, teacher, and intuition. To be truly humble is to recognize and acknowledge a power greater than ourselves whom we call the Great Spirit.

It is because of understanding in the eyes of the Great Spirit, that we are all equal. What makes us equal is the sacred breath of life the Great Spirit gives us. We are never to consider ourselves to be superior or inferior to anyone. Practicing Humility means we always consider our fellow humans before ourselves.

In the natural world, Ma'iingan expresses this Humility in great clarity. The Wolf bows his head not out of fear but out of humbleness, he humbles himself in our presence.

A Wolf that has hunted food will take the food back to the den to eat with the pack before he takes the first bite or he regurgitates all he has for the pups. Ma'iingan, an animal guide for true teaching.

Mikinaak (Snapping Turtle) represents Debwewin (Truth)

When the Great Spirit gave the Anishinaabe these laws, Mikinaak was present to ensure that the laws would never be forgotten or lost. There are thirteen markings on the back of the Mikinaak to denote the thirteen moons, which represent the Truth of one cycle of the earth's rotation around the sun, the four seasons. There are also 28 markings on Turtle's back to denote one cycle of the moon around earth.

These signs are confirmation of the Truth, which Mikinaak reflects. Mikinaak represents self-containment, Creative resource, Mother Earth, Adoptability, Love, Healing and Knowledge.

Photo Inserts

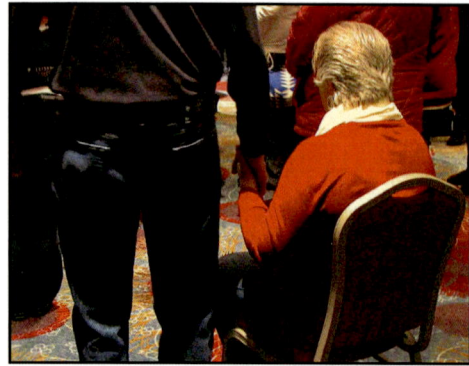

Photo Inserts

Part 4: PowerPoint Teachings

Early Teachings

The Path of Life

(See PowerPoint image insert at end of this section)

August 2006, 23 slides

The Direction of Growth (on the Medicine Wheel) starts in the East and moves clockwise with Emotional/Baby, Spiritual/Youth, Physical/Adult, and Mental/Elder.

The Eight Stages or Feelings of Development. Baby = trust and autonomy, Youth = initiative and accomplishment, Adult = identity and Intimacy, and Elder = generosity and integrity. Each stage must be completed.

(Path of Life PP03)

The Development of Growth. Again, starting in the East we begin with Self-worth, Self-Confidence, Self-Esteem, Self-Respect, Self-Image which all lead to a Solid Self-Concept.

The Infant Stage. A child is a gift from the Creator. A child comes into the world with the boundaries it needs in the areas of emotional, spiritual, physical, and mental. Their basic needs are water, food, trust, nurturing, love, and protection.

The primary caregiver is given the responsibility to provide and nurture these needs including protecting the boundaries of the aspects of growth. The infant must know that the people are good and trustworthy, and that the world is a good and safe place.

The child begins to trust the nurturing and caring from those around him/her. The child also begins to trust and believe that the world is a safe place.

The child starts to move towards the eight stages or feelings of development, (trust, autonomy, initiative, accomplishment, identity, intimacy, gener-

osity, integrity) and the child responds to those around him/her.

At the age of two, the child begins to explore and announce his/her independence. In the east, the baby quadrant is **Trust** which leads to **Autonomy** and independence. The child must be encouraged to become its own being.

At three to seven years, it is at this time when initiative must be encouraged for healthy development to take place. At this time **Initiative** is added to autonomy and independence, which flows from Trust. This state supports active imagination, role-playing, and pretending. There is a healthy testing of boundaries between imagination and reality.

At ages eight through eleven, the young person must learn to feel good for something and be good at doing something. **Accomplishment** is added to the former three which springs from trust. They need to receive praise and recognition for their accomplishments.

At ages 12 through 18, the young person must learn to belong and be somebody. This age group will need to get attention and praise for things well done. **Identity** is added to the litany of stages. At this age group they will begin to develop answers to the three questions: Who am I? Why am I here? Where am I going?

At ages 19 to 30 the young adult learns to share ideas with family and friends. They learn to be open with his/her innermost thoughts and feelings. **Intimacy** is added as they learn to form and maintain close relationships. All things gone well, we can then add, for older adults and elders, **generosity and integrity**.

Hurt Interferes. If we came from a troubled home, this often results in having a troubled self-image in life. We experience a disruption in one of the stages of our developmental process. The situations and feelings might be old, but they are not forgotten. They live in our attitudes, thoughts and feelings. They affect our day-to-day relationships and choices. The result is that our self-worth stayed fixed at a childhood level, a child in this environment begins to fear *feelings* and *emotions*.

Violation/Abuse Occurs. Hurt, fear, and pain affect our self-esteem. What we have of self-worth, self-respect, self-confidence, and self-image, is protected by our boundaries but is assaulted by emotional, psychological, spiritual, elderly, physical, mental, sexual, spousal, and child abuse. This sense of violation may lead to destruction of property or personal items.

(Path of Life PP15)

The Accumulation of Violations Begins to Occur. Trust and boundaries are damaged. There is confusion and we are withdrawn. The hurt, fear, and pain at the center feel more violations; emotional abuse, sexual abuse, threats, abandonment, neglect, betrayal, intimidation, verbal abuse, physical abuse, and psychological abuse. This creates a fear-based system.

The Individual Immediately Shuts Down. The person concentrates on securing and protecting the wound, and adopts three unspoken rules; don't feel, don't talk, and don't trust. There is hostility, denial, resentment, and anger. This develops that fear-based system.

The Person Develops a Solid Wall for protection to prevent further hurt fueled by resentment, depression, hostility, and anger, and they become emotionally unavailable to self/others.

The Person is Out of Harmony with Self. A person closes their self off from family, community and nation. There is fear and denial. There is resentment, shame, hostility, and anger. There are feelings of alienation, depression, numbness, powerlessness, hopelessness, helplessness, isolation, and they become withdrawn. There is a danger to give up on oneself and consider/commit suicide.

The Spirit is Wounded as the physical body continues to grow. Abandonment, depression, numbness, and sadness continue as well as resentment, fear, hostility, and anger. The person may begin to experiment with alcohol/drugs to ease the pain.

Anger is shared with resentment and toxic hostility. Abandonment, depression, loneliness, and sadness abound. A person does not feel or fear, they don't talk and they don't trust. The individual seeks to get their needs met.

Cycle of Life

Date Unknown, 18 slides

NOTE: *The images in this PP use the symbolism of the Medicine Wheel illustrated as a sweat lodge. It appears to me that in these early Teachings, Larry is speaking to Indians or using the Indian experience as an example or both. (Later he spoke to all four colors) No matter, hopefully it will help Indians understand themselves better, and help the non-Indian appreciate the experience and perhaps even relate to the teaching as their own.*

We begin with The Natural Cycle of Life. The Creator put into place a balanced system with two polarities, the seen and unseen, or the physical and spiritual worlds. Examples of that polarity-based system include; plus-minus, east-west, north-south, up-down, good-bad, man-woman, and boy-girl.

(Cycle of Life PP02)

Along the path of life, from child to adolescent, adult and elder, we were given by the Creator Natural Laws that include principles, laws, and values.

The cycle of life is an interconnected and interdependent system. The Creator gave us four Gifts of Life. The four gifts keep with the polarities, the seen are mental and physical, and the unseen are emotional and spiritual.

The eight stages or feelings of development are, starting in the east and moving clockwise, Trust, Autonomy, Initiative, Accomplishment, Identity, Intimacy, Generosity, and Integrity.

The path of life: Child, Adolescent, Adult and Elder. Direction of growth is mental, physical, emotional, and spiritual.

Natural Development. In addition to seen/unseen is Balance and Harmony. To get a Solid Self-Concept, we must have a strong Self-Image, Self-Assurance, Self-Confidence, Self-Esteem, Self-Respect, and Self-Worth.

(Cycle of Life PP07)

An Unnatural Cycle of Life begins with a deep hurt or pain. Disruption occurs and creates violation cycle in all forms. We are out of harmony and become dysfunctional.

This Unnatural Cycle affects us in two important ways, Historical Trauma and Generational Trauma. With Historical Trauma we are affected by a loss of land, a loss of Spiritual practices, the forceful removal of children, a loss of language, and the separation of families. Under Generational trauma, we experience a loss of tribal identity, a loss of unity of faith, a high rate of institutionalized children, the disruption of tribal economies, and the denigration of Indian life and culture.

(Cycle of Life PP09)

Sometimes this Unnatural Cycle includes an intrusion of alcohol and drugs and a loss of power and control. This can lead to elder abuse, abandonment, neglect, child abuse, sexual abuse, emotional abuse, psychological abuse, physical abuse, and destruction of property.

This then also leads to a disruption of the developmental process, or dysfunction from the hurt.

This unnatural cycle also leads to a violation of boundaries. This creates further pain, hurt, fear and anger. What boundaries have been violated? Were they physical, mental, emotional, or spiritual?

This unnatural cycle of hurt and pain may also lead to fear of anger, a legacy of unresolved grief, learned helplessness, spiritual bankruptcy, inherited apathy, and an incomplete grieving.

This pain, fear anger and hurt can also lead to the development of survival family roles and create a co-dependency system. These might include; the lost child, mascot, enabler, scapegoat, or family hero.

Anger. The risks involved in expressing anger include a fear of hurting others, a fear of rejection, fear of being hurt by others, fear of counter attack, fear of losing control, a fear that anger is not acceptable, and a fear of repeating bad experiences.

Grief. The types of losses caused by grief include the loss of a sense of security, of cultural identity, of death, of physical abuse, of sexual abuse, a loss of personal items, family, relationships, job, home, identity, and esteem.

In conclusion, this unnatural cycle leads to a disruption of the developmental process. Hurt, anger, fear and pain, lead to a fear of anger, incomplete grieving, inherited apathy, and a legacy of unresolved grief. Again we look to what boundaries have been violated? Were they physical, mental, emotional, or spiritual? This all leads to spiritual bankruptcy and we are out of harmony and balance.

Medicine Wheel/7 Teachings

Date Unknown, 21 slides

NOTE: *It is important to realize that medicine in this sense covers more than physical ailments, as most think of medicine, but rather medicine for all four of the aspects of life, Spiritual, Emotional, Mental, and Physical. What cures one, cures all. There must be balance for healing and for a healthy and good life.*

The Medicine Wheel

Medicine Wheel Teachings begin with the Four Sacred Directions. Each direction was given both physical and spiritual powers by the Creator who also put in place a balanced system and a polarity system. The Wheel always starts in the East, and then moves clockwise to south, west, and north.

The Medicine Wheel also has four Sacred Colors, again starting in the east with yellow, red, black and white. This also represents the four races of people.

The color placement may vary from tribe to tribe.

The Medicine Wheel has many layers too numerous for only one Teaching. Some others include the Cycle of Seasons: Spring, Summer, Fall, and Winter. The Cycle of Life: baby, youth, adult, and elder. The Four Directions of Growth: emotional, mental, physical, spiritual. And the Four Directions of Healing: Individual, Family, Community, Nation.

The Seven Sacred Rites refers to the seven points on the Medicine Wheel used in one of the most common prayer ceremonies. A prayer (often with pipe) is directed to each of the four directions, East, South, West and North, to Father Sky, to Mother Earth and to the Self, which is at the center of the Wheel.

(Med Wheel 7 Teach PP08)

The Seven Great Laws or Teachings

Love: The Anishinaabeg were to always act in LOVE. To love the Great Spirit the same way he loved His people, because it was the love of the Great Spirit that gave life. Children are to be loved, for children are a gift from the Great Spirit.

Respect: To RESPECT all life on Mother Earth. To show real respect was for the people to give of themselves for the benefit of all life. We are to respect the Elders and the Leaders who upheld the Sacred Laws of the Great Spirit.

Courage: To have COURAGE to always do that which was is right. To be proud of being Anishinaabe and never to deny the way of life the Great Spirit gave to us.

Honesty: To be HONEST to themselves. To live in the spirit of how they were created, and to never lie or gossip about one another.

Wisdom: To live in WISDOM is to know the gifts the Great Spirit gave to everyone. To use these gifts to build a family and community filled with caring, sharing, kindness, respect, and love for one another. When we know and use our gifts we become an instrument of the Great Spirit, helping to bring peace to the world.

Humility: Always to act in HUMILITY. One was to always think about their family, their fellow man, and their community before they thought of themselves. To know humility is to know that there is a Great Spirit and He is the creator of all life, and therefore He directs all life.

Truth: Always to seek the TRUTH. The truth lies in spirit. Prayer was to be done everyday at sunrise to give thanks to the Great Spirit for the gift of life. All gifts and each ceremony were given by the Great Spirit to the Anishinaabeg to help them find truth, the true meaning of their life, and existence. Living truth is living the Seven Great Laws.

Traditional Teachings
Traditional Native American Spirituality

April 2008, 18 slides

What Happened to Us?

The traditional way of life that our Ancestors developed for us as our heritage was disrupted by the massive upheaval and immeasurable losses that was perpetrated on our people. We as a people have experienced and endured phenomenally rapid changes in the past 100 to 150 years. We did not have the physical, mental or emotional understanding of the foreign concepts, including the diseases that were brought to our land.

When we were reeducated and forced to take on attitudes, behaviors and beliefs that were foreign to us, we lost the knowledge about how to think with a good mind and how we are to conduct ourselves. The most hideous thing that came out of being forced to take on those attitudes, behaviors and beliefs, was that we were taught to hate ourselves and each other so much, that we started to kill each other.

We as descendants are now faced with having to deal with the traumas that were perpetrated on our people.

What Am I? Who Am I? Why Am I Here?

The answers to these questions can be found in our ceremonies, traditions, beliefs, rites and customs. The traditional teachings are still as relevant today, as they were at the time of our Ancestors.

Our Elders have always encouraged us to attend the ceremonies and listen to the teachings. That's where the answers are for the many questions we may have about life. The teachings serve as blue prints for human behavior. They connect us to the teachers of the natural and spiritual world.

Most of us may have grown up without the teachings of our ceremonies, beliefs, rites and customs. This is why so many of us are struggling and confused as who we are and why we are here. Reclaiming our tradition is our source of confidence and self-esteem. The teachings will help change our attitude about what we want to do. It will help us realize that we are good people.

It is in the learning and coming to an understanding of yesterday that we can better prepare for the uncertainties of our tomorrow.

Traditional Native American Spirituality

All things in the Universe are related and have a purpose. The major contributors to human life are considered Sacred. They are Fire, Water, Air, Sun, Earth, Moon, Plants, and Animals.

In our Traditions we have given special names to these gifts. Grandfather – Sun, Father – Sky, Mother – Earth, Grandmother – Moon, Brothers and Sisters – Plants and Animals, First Medicine – Water, and Fire.

In our Traditional Ceremonies through historical stories, we believe the Creator put plants and Animals on Earth so humans could live. Human Beings are pitiful because we are the only species that depend on all the others. Because the plants and animals also depend on the Sun, Earth, Cosmos and Water, they are considered brother and sister.

Those that were assigned by the Creator to give their life for the human survival knew this. Humans, plants, birds, fish and animal spirits communicate with each other through the Creator. Humans have not always understood our responsibility to the Sacred things we are dependent on. The Creator sent the human beings a teacher to teach them about the plants, birds, four-legged and fish. Humans had to learn respect.

All of the Sacred gifts from the Creator are considered alive and have Spirits. All of these gifts are to be treated with the respect they deserve. All things we are given in this life are borrowed. Nothing belongs to us. Even our children don't belong to us. They belong to everyone. We as a people believe that our responsibility while here on this planet is to take care of our Earth Mother, in a very sacred way.

The land and all things we get from our Earth Mother are Sacred. All Native people have a creation story. All Native tribes call Mother Earth "Turtle Island." In the stories it mentions the destruction of the first earth, because the people did not respect the gifts the Creator gave them. All the animals, birds, insects and the fish have their own tribes.

Because we are pitiful and not pure, we have been given Sacred Herbs, medicines to purify ourselves and other things to use before we pray. Every-

thing Sacred we pray with is always purified (through ceremony) before we are allowed to use it. The four medicines are: **Tobacco** – (Asemaa) – offering; **Cedar** – purification – medicine (health); **Sweet Grass** – purification; and **Sage** - purification – medicine.

The center of all Spirituality is to know humility and gratitude for all we have been given. We are to show this humility and gratitude through prayer. There are prayers in everything we do. Our Traditional Spirituality is practiced in our everyday lives. Spirituality is a way of life. We are to make tobacco offerings every morning and evening.

We have been given Sacred Items to borrow and use to pray. Each item has come to people in different ways at different intervals. They include the Eagle Story, the Drum Story: Water, Hand, and Traditional. The Pipe Story; Rattles and Whistles, and the Sweat Lodge, Long House, and Shake Tent.

Humans of all races are interrelated and all have a purpose on Earth. The four races are: Yellow, Red, Black, and White.

Dewe'igan: The Heartbeat of Mother Earth

October 2012, 15 slides

"The drum has always been a part of the Anishinaabe culture. "The people's history can be heard in the songs. Preserving the songs means preserving Anishinaabe lifeway's and worldviews." ~ Gichi-Ma'iingan

Dewe'igan (The Drum)

The animal that provides the hide does so with intention and purpose. The spirit of the animal nation lives in the drum. The honor and respect we have for the drum also honors the four legged, winged, swimmers, crawlers and insects.

The tree that contributes the wood for the frame does so with intention and purpose. The spirit of the plant nation lives in the drum. The honor and respect we give the drum honors the trees, flowers and grasses.

The stone in the heart of the drum asks to be part of the drum so we will remember the stone nation. With the honor and respect we give the drum, we honor and respect the soil, water and air. When we use the drum, prayers from the web of life are sent to the star nation connecting Mother Earth and Father Sky.

The purpose of the stone is so we can hold the spirit of the foundation of the web of life. The stone is the first Order of Being upon which all other things depend on for their lives. The plant world; trees, grasses, and flowers receive life from the rocks, water and air.

Plants are the second Order of Being in the web of life upon which the animal nation depends. The third Order of Being in the web of life is the animal who gives its own flesh so their younger brother, the human, can live. These are the four Orders of Being in the web of life, each interwoven with the other, interconnected in the one.

The drum, as beautiful as it is, is not a decorative object. It is alive just as we are.

It feels the cold, heat, damp and the dry. We have to take care of it, feed it, touch it and treat it with love and respect. It will last for many generations when we treat it with care.

We have to protect it from extreme temperatures and humidity. High humidity will dull the tone. Extreme low humidity tightens the hide giving it a high tone and can split or crack the drumhead. It is to always be wrapped in insulating layers of protection and kept in a safe place.

Just like humans, each drum has its unique voice and vibration for the simple reason that each animal and tree, from which it is made, has their own unique medicines, their spirit being part of the drum. There are many teachings of the drum, one can study the drum for a lifetime and never be aware of all the lessons that will be revealed as one grows spiritually.

Before we use the drum, it is always prepared with a cleansing ceremony and prayer to the Seven Directions. We do this to purify and cleanse the people, place and things. The smudging brings awareness of the sacred and should be performed with sensitivity and respect.

This ceremony offers thanks to the Grandmothers and Grandfathers of the four directions. The order of honoring starts with the east because the sun begins in the east, always rotating clockwise so we follow the path of the sun, then to Mother Earth, Father Sky and finally to the Great Mystery within all things.

The drum's roundness is considered sacred. The drum is sacred not only in its sound but in the deep wisdom it silently conveys for those who become aware. The drum's silent voice waits to be released into the presence of not only the ears of humans, but also the rocks, grasses, trees, and animals. All of life becomes aware of its sacred power.

The drum teaches us to listen to the whisper of the spirit wind in our heart, which connects us with Mother Earth, Father Sky, the Star Nation, the Grandmothers, and the Grandfathers, who are the spirit keepers of the four directions. Most importantly, it connects us with the Great Mystery that lives within us. These are the Seven Directions.

There are many ways to use the drum. It can be used for sending prayers and connecting with the star nation. It allows us to receive power, wisdom and healing energy. It is used to remove blockages of energy flow, learn the power of deep passion, and it carries the energy of love.

The Four Elements Essential for Life

December 2013, 23 slides

The Four Elements Essential for Life

The Fire of the sun warms Mother Earth. Mother Earth provides nourishment for all of creation. The Water and Air sustain life.

In smudging, the shell represents the water element. The sacred herb represents the earth element. The spark to light it represents the fire element. The smoke represents the air element.

(Four Elements, PP03)

Fire is in the East, Earth is in the south, Water is in the West, and Air is in the North.

Guardians of the Four Elements

To the East is Fire whose guardian is Grandfather Sun, the power of heat and light. To the South is Earth whose guardian is Mother Earth, the power of growth and healing. To the West is Water whose guardian is Grandmother Moon, the power to purify and renew. To the North is Air whose guardian is Father Sky, the power of the breath of life.

The Fire Element

The spark of fire creates warmth from inside out. It symbolizes the creative spark and the element of change. It's expressed through inspired acts of intuitive impulses. It's a natural urge that's associated with being inspired, engaged, alive and motivated. Its growth kindles the joy for living and its energy carries us to play, explore and to express ourselves. We need fire to be passionate about what we are doing, it helps burn away self-doubt and gives us the energy for acting on what makes us alive.

Excessive Fire Energy

Displays itself as; anxious, restless, stressed, controlling, jittery, impatient, and impulsive.

Low Fire Energy

Displays itself as fatigued, lethargic, unmotivated, and difficulty concentrating.

Balance the fire Element

Sit around a campfire, or light candles.

The Earth Element

Harnesses our innate talents. It symbolizes abundance, sustenance, grounding and stability. Makes us more practical, we tend to carefully seek out situations for ourselves. When we're balanced with the earth element we feel more competent. We're more able to move forward toward more tangible goals. Helps us to feel more embodied within.

Excessive Earth Energy

Displayed by poor boundaries, impatient, impractical, and disrespectful.

Low Earth Energy

Displays itself as insecure, overly dependent on others, looking for attention, seeking affection, and trouble saying no.

Balance the Earth Element

Walk the dog, work in the garden, walk in the woods, walk by the lake, rocks, or have houseplants.

The Water Element

Purifies and cleanses. It symbolizes the emotional realm, healing, dreaming and flowing. We feel its power when tears well up unexpectedly and we experience a great release. Opening up to the water element in all our emotions, we discover ways to honor them and help us come out of stagnation and lethargy. Water balance helps us find our own pathway in life.

Excessive Water Energy

Displays a volatile temperament, stubborn, willful, and persistent.

Low Water Energy

Displays melancholy, moody, miserable, sad, and distressed.

Balance the Water Element

Dip your hands in water, swim, have an aquarium, walk in the rain, or soak in a bath.

The Air Element

It symbolizes the realm of thought, learning, knowledge, communication and all things mental. It also symbolizes breath. It's expressed through our thoughts and our nervous system. When air is balanced our mind is free and flexible. It lets us mentally travel and explore, allowing new ideas to widen our horizon. It helps to break through old ways of thinking including old ideas that don't serve us anymore.

Air brings emotional detachment and helps us make good decisions. When the air is moving it can makes us more lively, sociable, curious, alive and is the driving force to want to learn more.

Excessive Air Energy

Displays itself as muddy thinking, being unfocused, negative thinking, being easily distracted, and overly imaginative.

Low Air Energy

Displays itself as shortness of breath, trouble releasing waste, digestive problems, and trouble communicating.

Balance the Air Element

Use a fan, stand in the wind, or listen to wind chimes.

The Four Basic Elements

To the East is Fire, the South is Earth, the West is Water, and the North is Air. These elements balance and nourish each other.

A Review

To the East are candles, eagle, and tobacco. To the South are rocks, wolf, and cedar. To the West are water, bear, and sage. To the North is a fan, buffalo, and sweet grass.

(Four Elements, PP23)

Anishinaabe Spirituality: The Four Sacred Medicines

August 2013, 13 slides

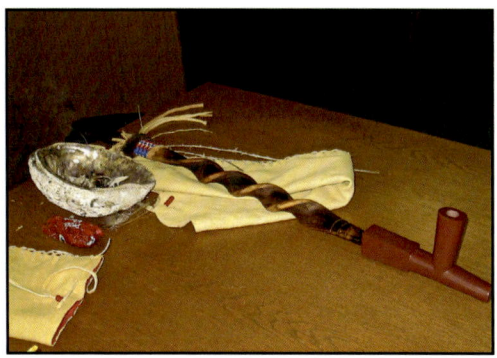

There are many aspects to our spirituality.

Smudging is one ceremony we use frequently. It is a cleansing ceremony used to open most of the activities at a spiritual gathering. It is common to use tobacco, sage, sweet grass and/or cedar.

Tobacco:

Tobacco is used for various purposes. It is offered before we take anything from Mother Earth. It is believed to open the door from the physical world to the spirit world.

Sage:

Sage is believed to be a masculine plant. It reduces or eliminates negative energy.

Sweet grass:

Sweet grass is believed to be a feminine plant that teaches kindness because it bends without breaking. It is considered to be the hair of Mother Earth, we show respect to her by braiding it. It is used to attract positive energy.

Cedar:

Cedar offers protection and grounding. It can be placed at the entrance to a home. It is used in a sweat lodge. It can be brewed as a tea or it can be used for extra grounding in shoes for daily wear.

The smoke from these four medicines is fanned with an Eagle Feather. When we smudge, we first cleanse our hands as if we were washing our hands. Then we draw the smoke over our heart, mouth, eyes and to the rest of the body.

Pipe Ceremony

A pipe ceremony is a thanking ceremony. It always begins with a smudging. Everything and everyone in the ceremony is cleansed with the smudging.

There are two parts to a pipe: the bowl and the stem. They are put together only for the occasion of the ceremony. The bowl is the feminine part, made of the stone people of Mother Earth. The stem is the male part, made of the standing people of Mother Earth.

When they are put together, the spirit of the pipe is alive, the smoke is its breath. After it is cleansed with the sacred medicines, it is filled with tobacco. A pinch of tobacco is offered to each of the seven directions with a prayerful request for their participation, then it is put into the bowl.

A pipe ceremony is often requested for a reason. The Elder will share the reason with the participants. The smoke from the pipe is not to be inhaled, it is encouraged to ascend to the Creator by drawing the smoke through the stem. The Elder washes his head and body with the smoke as he prays.

The Elder offers the pipe to the East, then to the South, West and finally to the North. It is offered to the Sky (above), to Mother Earth (below) and to the Creator (the center). Between each direction the pipe is rotated to indicate the change in direction.

Participants take turns in drawing the smoke from the pipe and praying to the Creator. It returns to the Elder in a clockwise direction. The Elder will then empty any remains in the pipe bowl, clean it, take it apart, wrap the parts and then returns them to his medicine bundle.

The Seven Fires Prophecy

December 2010, 29 Slides

The way of the mind that was brought to our land has created great danger to our Earth Mother.

For most of us today, life has become a nightmare as we struggle just to survive in our search for answers to questions like: How did we get to be this way? What happened to us? Perhaps, the answers we are seeking lie in our past.

The Elders tell us if we do not learn from our past, we are doomed to repeat those things of the past.

The Elders tell us that we have created so many excuses and placed our blame on external things for a long time, and now we're waiting for life to happen. Like waiting for: the right job, the right partner, or for others to get well.

The Elders say that this has caused us to miss out on living our true lives.

The Elders are telling us that we are the one's we've been waiting for.

A long time ago Seven Prophets came to our people and gave us seven prophecies or predictions about what was going to happen in the future. The Seven fires of the prophecies represent key spiritual teachings.

The Seventh Fire Prophecy, A Place of Understanding

Ni-gan-na-jim-mo-wi-non (Prophecies) Niizhwaaso ishkodaykawn (Seventh Fire)

Each of the Prophecies represented an era of time in our history as Anishinaabeg. All of the prophecies have come to pass except the last one. We are now in the time of Seventh Fire. The task we have before us now is to include the other three colors of the human race and come together to choose the road of cooperation.

The Elders tell us, if we don't do this there will be no Eighth Fire. We are the Seventh Fire of the Seven Fire Prophecies.

We are now standing at a crossroad where we are faced with a choice between two roads. One is the Black Road of technology and overdevelopment leading to catastrophe.

The other is the Red Road of spirituality and respect for the earth. This puts us back to the time of the Fourth Fire Prophecy. In the time of the Fourth Fire Prophecy two prophets came to our people as one. The first prophet told of the coming of the light skinned race.

The first prophet said we would know our future by the face the light skinned race wears. If they come wearing the face of brotherhood, there will come a time of wonderful change for generations to come. They will bring new knowledge and articles that can be joined with our knowledge; in this way two nations will join to make a mighty nation.

This new nation will be joined by two more so that the four will be the mightiest nation of all. We will know the face of brotherhood if they come carrying no weapons and carrying only their knowledge and a handshake. The other prophet said: Beware if they come wearing the face of death. Be careful because the face of brotherhood and the face of death look very much alike.

Beware if they come in suffering they can fool you, their hearts will be filled with greed for the riches of this land. If they are indeed our brothers, let them prove it, do not accept them in total trust. You shall know the face they wear is one of death if the rivers run with poison and fish become unfit to eat. You will know them by these things.

We know that the prophecy of the second prophet has come to pass. Our wisdom keepers say, in the time of the Seventh Fire there will rise a new people "osh-ki-bi-madi-zeeg" who will emerge from the clouds of illusion. They will retrieve the old ways that have been lost; they will remember the original instructions that will help them find the strength of the ways of the circle.

As the osh-ki-bi-madi-zeeg begin trusting in the way of the "Circle" they will no longer need the selfish voice of the "ego", they will begin to trust their inner voice and the "Sacred Fire" will be lit again. Every one of us is needed to participate in this time of the Seventh Fire.

We are being called to return to the peaceful ways of our ancestors in order to stop the destruction of the earth before we end up getting destroyed. We are being asked to put our "differences" aside and start speaking for our Earth Mother and the Great Spirit who's in everything and in all people.

We are to create a spiritual circle where we join the material and spiritual together to take care of our Earth Mother in a spiritual way. To do this we are to include the other three colors of the human family so we can start working together to choose the right road and to be of one mind. The destruction of our sacred land must stop before it destroys our entire way of life.

The Elders are telling us that now is the time for us to let go and forgive all that's happened to us. Without forgiveness we will not be able to think clearly. They tell us that we need to be strong and healthy in order to be able to teach the *road of cooperation and spiritual understanding* before it is too late.

As the Seventh Fire, we are the movement toward decolonization; we are now finding a voice for our concerns and identity. The Seventh Fire is not just a time of reclaiming our spiritual teachings; it is a time for us to use our teachings to help correct the imbalance felt in the great circle of life. The Elders say that this is not just a revitalization movement; it is more like we have arrived.

More and more of us are now listening and learning about the teachings of the Seven Fire Prophecies and we are starting to make our concerns felt throughout the whole web of life. The stronger and healthier we are as spiritual warriors the more we will be able to give of ourselves to our continual healing and the healing of our Earth Mother.

Being stronger and healthier makes it easier for us to do our part in the universe, to serve our people and for each of us to fulfill our personal vision. In retracing the footsteps of our ancestors we will find a new way of living in harmony with our Earth Mother. This is a time for healing, preparation and purification for all of us.

The Seventh Prophet

The Seventh Prophet was different from the other prophets; he was younger and had a strange light in his eyes. He said: "In the time of the Seventh Fire a new people will emerge."

They will retrace their steps to find what was left behind. Their steps will take them to the Elders to ask them for guidance for their journey. But, many of the Elders have fallen asleep and they will wake up with nothing to offer. Some of them have gone home to the spirit world. Some of them will be silent because no one is asking anything of them.

We are to be careful in how we approach the Elders. Our task as the Seventh Fire will not be easy. If we remain strong in our quest for our ceremonies there will be a rebirth for us as Anishinaabeg. The Seventh Fire will be lit again.

The Prophet of the Fourth Fire spoke of a time when two nations will join to make a mighty nation. He spoke of the coming of the light skinned race and the faces they could be wearing. It's obvious from our history it was not the face of brotherhood.

The mighty nation spoken of in the Fourth Fire was never formed. The Elders say if we the people of the earth wear the face of brotherhood we might be able to deliver our society from the road of destruction. We can make the two roads that represent two clashing worlds to form a mighty nation, a nation that will be guided by respect for all living things.

We are being asked to speak as one voice to awaken the people to the catastrophic consequences we face if we don't change the way we relate to each other and our Earth Mother. The "Red Road" is a phrase we are given so we can walk in balance and to live right by following the rules of the Creator.

In experiencing the Red Road we learn the lesson of the physical life or of being human. Walking in balance is more than just a physical action; it also encompasses our mental, emotional and spiritual aspects of our being. We are to call on the Wisdom and Power of the way of the Circle to follow the way of the spirit so we can walk in balance and harmony with all beings.

Sweat Lodge Teachings

Sweat Lodge (1) August 2009, 50 slides

The Original Creation: Aadizookaan (A Sacred Story, Legend or Myth)

My Elders say that there are no experts on anything. There are only people who have knowledge on certain ceremonies. The path is not always clear. Some of us lose our way. But if we walk the good path, when we commit to the values and fulfill our goals, the meaning of life will find us.

Mino-Bimaadiziwin (The Good Life)

A long time ago our people lived a life of total submission to the Great Spirit.

They lived by the teachings of the Grand Medicine Lodge.

Midewiwin (The Grand Medicine Lodge)

The Elders say when the Great Spirit finished creating the Universe and life on Earth He gave the people Sacred Legends, which are contained in the Order of the Grand Medicine Lodge teachings of life.

The Grand Medicine Lodge ceremony provides the spiritual strength for our physical wellbeing to become whole and balanced with creation. Our Ceremonies and Rituals such as the sweat lodge, fasting, healing, naming, vision quest, are all contained in the Grand Medicine Lodge teachings.

Principles, Laws and Values

Our people understood and lived by the Principles, Laws and Values, that the Great Spirit put in place to run the Universe. They were put in place for all forms of life to abide by. They are designed to help us live in balance and in harmony.

Circles and Cycles

Life is designed to grow in a system of circles and cycles. Everything is interconnected, interdependent, and interrelated in a balanced system that has two polarities. Everything in creation follows this path in a great circle of life. This evolving system is also designed with a mechanism that is constantly changing.

Time of Great Healing:

Every person is needed to accomplish this great healing. We must all get involved to see what the Great Spirit wants us to do. We need to help each other in this time of healing.

We Seek Healing to:

Stop inflicting pain on others and ourselves; To quiet the tears of the children; to confront our shame; to forgive the unforgiveable; to find our identity; to find our meaning and purpose; and to fulfill our spiritual emptiness.

We want the "Good Mind" to be able to:

See the power of truth; to consult with an Elder; to seek the counsel of the Great Spirit; to make good decisions for our children, families and communities; and to journey the Red Road.

Ceremonies

A long time ago the Great Spirit gave our ancestors all the knowledge and wisdom about how to live and conduct themselves. Our ancestors did not have books so the Great Spirit gave them Ceremonies. Ceremonies are our first duty. They are our access to the unseen world. These teachings are as relevant for us today as they were back then with our ancestors. **The Sweat Lodge is one of the Ceremonies.**

Sweat Lodge Teaching

We Participate in the Sweat Lodge Ceremony for:

Purification of the body and mind from toxins; for centering and balance; for the Spiritual significance; for the social and cultural experience; for sobriety; for healing to repair the damage done to our spirit, and for personal experience.

How the Sweat Lodge Came to the People

A long time ago when the people were living a balanced and peaceful life with the animals, plants, Earth Mother and all living things, life was good. Then something happened, a liquid called a *mind changer* was introduced to our people.

The "Mind Changer"

When the people took in this *mind changer* and became consumed by it, everything started to change. There was drinking, fighting, cheating, blaming, lying, stealing, and resenting each other. There was jealousy, dishonesty, hostility, anger and fear.

The Little Boy and the Grandfathers

One day a little boy listened to his heart because he could not stand all the ugliness and meanness that was all around him. He began searching for something to help his people. He began asking everyone that would listen. "What can we do to stop what is happening to the people?" Sadly, no one knew what to do.

Finally, he found some people that had the same concern, they told him, "Go to the Elders, they have been here the longest, if anybody would know they would." The little boy started his search for the Elders. It was hard to find an Elder, because many of the Elders were so disenfranchised. Many had gone on to the Spirit World.

Many had forgotten their wisdom and were unable to help. Some pointed to the wrong direction because they had lost their way. Some remained silent because of their fear and shame for not knowing their tradition. Some remained silent because no one asked them for their wisdom.

After searching long and hard, he finally found some Elders who were willing to listen. The Elders said, "We have been waiting for you for a long time." The little boy asked, "Can you help me find some way to help the people?" The Elders said, "We will help, we will teach you."

The Elders told him, "This is what we are going to do. We will find a place for you where it's quiet and where you can be alone. You will fast and deprive your body of the life-giving forces, (food and water) for four days and four nights. In lessening your physical side, the spiritual side will come into dominance."

They said, "Fasting will purify your body and mind and make you receptive to the messages from the spirit world. A vision will come to you to serve as a guiding light for the questions you seek. The vision will give your life its purpose and direction."

The little boy did as he was told and began his fasting.

At the end of the fourth day, the little boy was very weak and kept falling into a deep sleep. Then, the Oshkaabewis (spirit helper) came down from the sky and took him away. The Oshkaabewis took him past the moon, the sun and the star nation. They traveled until they came to a big lodge in the sky.

The Oshkaabewis left the little boy there. He was very scared. Then he heard some voices coming from inside the lodge, the voices called to him "biindigen (come in), we have been waiting for you." Inside the lodge were seven Grandfathers. Each Grandfather had a teaching to give the little boy.

The Grandfathers spoke as if their words were sent directly from their minds to the mind of the little boy. One Grandfather said, "You were sent by the Great Spirit to take a special gift back to the people. The Great Spirit is disturbed by the way the people are living."

A vessel sat in the front of the Grandfathers. One Grandfather said, "Look into the vessel."

When he did, he saw a beautiful tree, the tree of life.

One Grandfather said, "The Tree of Life is the life of the people. The Great Spirit planted a Sacred Tree for all the people of the earth for their healing, power, wisdom and security. The roots of the tree spread deep into the body of Mother Earth, its branches reach upward like hands praying to Father Sky."

Another Grandfather said, "The fruits of the Tree are the good things the Great Spirit gave to the people. It expresses and represents meaning. Meaning helps to provide purpose and understanding. The Tree is capable of providing enough meaning for a lifetime of reflection. It shows the path to love, forgiveness, compassion, patience, wisdom, honor, courage, respect, humility and justice."

And another Grandfather told him, "We know the people have wandered away from the protection of the Tree and have forgotten how to seek its nourishment. They have turned against it and are attempting to destroy it. They have lost their power and ceased to dream dreams and see visions."

Yet another Grandfather said, "They are now quarreling at each other and are unable to tell the truth or deal with each other honestly. They have forgotten how to survive in their own land and have become filled with jealousy, anger and hate. They are poisoning themselves and all they touch. The Sacred teachings are being twisted to imply conflict."

The Grandfather continued, "The Ceremonies are becoming oriented to gain spiritual favor for personal power or selfish reasons. Elitism is becoming the example for the young people to follow instead of peace, humility, respect and generosity. A great sorrow has fallen on the people."

Another Grandfather said, "It was foretold that these things would come to pass if the people did not listen. But, the Tree will never die, and as long as the Tree lives, the people will live. The time has come for the people to wake up from a long drugged-like sleep."

Then another Grandfather continued, "They will begin timidly at first, but then with a great urgency they will once again begin searching for the teachings. For the people to become healthy again, they must seek to develop themselves spiritually and find the balance between the physical and spiritual worlds."

And another Grandfather said, "This knowledge and wisdom we're giving you has always been carefully guarded and preserved in the hearts and minds of the wise, humble and dedicated Elders that managed to keep the Ceremonies alive. They will guide anyone who is honestly and sincerely seeking."

Then each Grandfather reached into the vessel and touched the little boy so he would not forget the teachings. The Seven Grandfathers explained every detail of the special gift on how it is to be made and how the ceremony is to be conducted.

One Grandfather said, "It is time to take the teachings back to the people."

The Oshkaabewis took the boy back to his people. When the boy woke up he was very weak, so weak he could hardly move. After a while he stretched his arm out and felt something, it was a plant. He put the plant in his mouth and ate it. He began to regain his strength and ate some more.

When the boy was strong enough he sat up. He watched the sun as it was coming up in the east and it cast a shadow down the hill to a lodge. He got up and went to find the Elders to tell them about the vision and the special gift he was given. The Elders listened. They knew the boy was given a special gift.

When the little boy saw the Lodge reflected down the hill, he remembered the special gift he had been given. He explained to the Elders about his vision and the instructions of the special gift he was given by the Seven Grandfathers.

(Sweat Lodge 1 PP43)

The Elders said, always remember to offer tobacco as a thanksgiving before taking anything from the Earth Mother.

The Lodge is to be made of sapling of the willow tree. Humans will use only the eastern doorway. There shall be four rings of willow placed on the lodge. It is to have four doors for the spirits of the four directions. The center shall have a shallow pit that represents the womb of Mother Earth.

A person will be given the gift of conducting the ceremony. Outside the lodge a path shall be made to the fire pit. A fire keeper will take care of the Grandfathers (rocks) that will be used for the ceremony. The fire keeper will instruct the participants in the order they will enter. The fire pit shall be surrounded by a crescent-shape altar.

There are different types of sweat lodges. Different Tribes have sweat lodges and may also run them differently. People within the same Tribe may build and run their sweat lodge differently as well.

Four Aspects of the human being

Our emotional center is a valuable part of us. Spirit energy moves in a clockwise direction. It's connected to our physical wellbeing, our thinking, (mental) and our spirituality.

(Sweat Lodge 1 PP48)

Unfortunately, many of us needed to shut down the emotional part of ourselves to survive certain situations in our lives. We shut down the part of us that feels anger, sadness, fear, joy, love and our access to our spirituality.

Today, a lot of us are seeking the sweat lodge to heal from the pain caused by the many years of drinking, drugging or from all the immeasurable losses we experienced.

Construction and Significance of the Sweat Lodge (2)

August 2009, 38 slides

(Sweat lodge 2 PP02,05,06)

Symbolism

Symbols have always been a major part of our culture. They offer a complete and reverent language of life, nature and spirit. The language is unmatched in its depth and power. It derives power from the fact that we view all things - animate or inanimate - as possessing a spirit.

Symbolic meanings play an integral part in our lives. Everything in the universe holds a deeper meaning. The pictographs of our ancestors convey profound beliefs and perception. All objects and beings in creation deserve our attention and respect. Our people view symbols through the creative and imaginative side of the left-brain.

All elements in nature are designed to be interconnected, interrelated and interdependent with each other. Sacred Laws provide the natural flow in the universe and are the balance between the physical and the spiritual world. We are to put the frame of reference for our thinking on Mother Earth to help us understand the natural order that runs the Universe.

Medicine Wheel

The Medicine Wheel is the original symbol given for us to guide our lives in a good way. Everything the Great Spirit created is contained in the ancient symbol to help us understand things we can or cannot quite see yet. Nature is its own blue print.

The difference between nature, and us, is we are designed with free will.

We have the ability to make choices and decisions. The situations and conditions in our lives are always from the results of the choices and decisions we make. Our responsibility is to walk in balance with the Sacred Laws of Creation. We are to pray and observe nature to learn about the physical and spiritual laws that run the universe. We were given the gift of bawaajigewin (vision quest) for seeking spiritual advice and direction.

We must fast to purify the body and mind to make us receptive for messages from the spirit world. Our ancestors developed knowledge, wisdom and power through bawaajiganan (dreams) and the way of the circle for our heritage. The knowledge, wisdom and power are in our ceremonies to help us to live in a good way. The purpose of conducting the ceremonies is to encourage an attitude of continuous growth.

Ceremonies

Add meaning, depth, dignity, a time of reflection and it brings people together. They help us remember the original teaching and creation. Ceremonies help us to successfully move through all the stages of life. They are also tools that remind us to keep the good feelings that help us in this reality to walk the Red Road.

We all have this innate knowledge that will direct us to greater understanding of self. This is why our ceremonies are our first duty. This is the form of psychology our people use to reach the inner person (spirit) using specific symbols, sounds, movements and colors.

Madoodiswan (Sweat Lodge)

Sweat Lodges

Each is unique in itself. They vary greatly from tribe to tribe, region to region, even within a single community by the spiritual leaders. All have a universal purpose of spiritual renewal and purification. Sweat Lodges are used for numerous occasions from sacred matters to social events.

The major purpose of a sweat lodge is for spiritual renewal and purification. The lodge for this presentation is just one of many different versions.

The design of the Sweat Lodge is patterned after the Medicine Wheel. It is designed to follow a circular and cyclic pattern. It is also designed to give us feedback, be it positive or negative. It is where our ceremonies, songs, beliefs, rituals, traditions, customs and nations originated.

Madoodiswan

The Sweat Lodge is usually placed in a location that will facilitate communication with the spirit world. It is built with great care and respect to the environment to match its' use. It is used for ceremonial prayer purpose. The place provides a necessary ceremonial setting for spiritual connection, healing, purification, as well as fasting.

The ceremony begins when a place is chosen for the sweat lodge. Every part of the lodge has symbolic significance. Start by digging two holes about one foot deep and two feet apart to the north, two to the east, two to the south, and two to the west, for a total of eight holes. Put tobacco in each hole before putting each willow pole in the hole.

The Southern West pole represents the words and wisdom of the ancestors.

The Northern West pole represents death and dreams of the past.

The Western South pole represents words which have been spoken.

The Western North pole represents old dreams.

The Eastern South pole represents words which will be spoken.

The Eastern North pole represents new dreams.

The Southern East pole represents the word which needs to be spoken.

The Northern East pole represents birth, rebirth and new beginnings.

Placing the poles in the ground symbolizes the role that Mother Earth plays in the healing, purifying and obtaining a spiritual experience. She is our first Mother. She takes care of all our physical needs.

(Sweat lodge 2 PP22)

Four Spirit doors are aligned with the Four Sacred Directions. Only the human being uses the eastern door. The two poles from the North and the two on the South are bent and tied together. This symbolically represents the connection between words and dreams. The two poles East and two on the West are bent together and tied symbolizing the continuity and harmony, and represent the continuous cycle of birth and rebirth. Connecting the East and west symbolizes the dreams of the ancestors which are directly connected to the dreams of the future.

(Sweat lodge 2 PP23)

The door faces the direction of the rising sun, which symbolizes the rebirth of the participants to enter and emerge from the lodge. Four rings of willow are placed from bottom up and represent the four cycles of life and Creation. A pit is dug in the center of the lodge for the hot rocks (Grandfathers).

(Sweat lodge 2 PP24)

The sweat lodge is a full circle with both physical and spiritual aspects.

Above the circle sweat is Seen World…Physical and Mental, below the surface to complete the circle is the Unseen World…spiritual and emotional. The rings symbolize the four cycles of life as well as the four aspects of development. (Circular rings round the sweat to hold the 8 poles together)

(Sweat lodge 2 PP25)

The Sweat Lodge symbolizes the womb of Mother Earth

Grandmother watches over the lodge. The lodge is covered with blankets or canvas.

The door faces the direction of the rising sun. The earth from the pit is a place for the altar. The rocks are called Grandfathers, and they are considered the wise ones, sometimes called the bones of Mother Earth.

(Sweat lodge 2 PP26)

The inside the lodge resembles the Four Quadrants of the Medicine Wheel.

Some refer to them as the four hills of life that corresponds to the four levels of growth. Some refer to the inside as the ribs of Mother Earth.

When a request is made for a sweat, the preparation begins long before the participants arrive. Tobacco is offered by the fire keeper for the wood, rocks, and water that are gathered for the ceremony. Tobacco is offered to the four directions, Father Sky, Mother Earth and placed in the fire pit.

The Four Basic Elements, Fire, Water, Air and Earth are all present. The wood is placed in the fire pit, and then the Grandfathers are placed on the wood and start the fire. Tobacco is offered to the Rocks, signifying we are related to them as we are related to all of creation. They are heated for several hours before the ceremony begins. The crescent shape symbolizes Grandmother Moon.

(Sweat lodge 2 PP28)

The Sacred Path from the fire to the shallow pit in the center of lodge is the pathway of life, and represents the beginning of time, the beginning of life, to the end of life.

The shallow pit represents the place of the Great Mystery's power, which symbolizes the center of everything. The Sacred Fire is the fire that never dies. It represents the light of the world, eternity, equality, unity and life, and it symbolizes the sun.

The Sweat Lodge encompasses both the beginnings and endings. It symbolizes birth, death and rebirth. It utilizes all the powers of the universe and the things that grow from the earth, fire, water and air.

The Sacred Fire symbolizes the first light, and represents Grandfather Sun. It symbolizes the same fire that is at the core of Mother Earth, the source of all life and power.

The Rocks are the symbols of endurance, the same way Mother Earth endures.

They absorb the power of Fire. The rock is to earth as bone is to the flesh.

The Rocks are referred to as Grandfathers. They are alive and must be treated with respect. They are placed in the shallow pit. The pit represents the place where all things come from and return.

The Gifts

To the East - the Gift of Innocence and the Law of Control over self, which provides the freedom of choice, to choose positive or negative thoughts or actions.

To the South - the Gift of Freedom and the Law of Order, this is the nature of creation, which is how things happen and it's the sacred balance between the physical, mental, spiritual and the universe.

To the West - the Law of Balance which is contained in the natural cycle of life to which we are responsible to restore and maintain balance.

To the North - the Law of Harmony combines the Four Sacred Laws of Creation. Together they provide control, order, balance and harmony in creation.

These are the Natural Laws that no one escapes.

Gifts of the Four Directions

Waabanong (East), Childhood, Birth, Renewal, Hope, Illumination, **Ziigwan** (Springtime)

Zhaawanong (South), Youth, Discipline, Development, Compassion, Sensitivity, **Niibin** (Summertime)

Ningaabiiwanong (West) Adult, Introspection, Reflection, Silence, Contemplation,

Humility, **Dagwaagin** (Falltime)

Giiwedinong (North), Elder, Wisdom, Interpreting, Fulfillment, Knowledge, Intuition, **Biboon** (Wintertime)

Participating in a Sweat Lodge Ceremony (3)

August 2009, 41 slides

(Sweat Lodge 3 PP01, Sweat Lodge 3 PP05-08)

Obaashiing Traditional University

As descendants of a people whose culture was denied, most of us have never been taught our cultural traditions. Those of us that had some exposure to our traditions may have misplaced our spirituality.

But, it cannot be said that we have lost our traditions, because our grandpas and grandmas are within us. They have been waiting for us to come to this place in time, where they will wake up to help us in our quest for a good life.

The ceremonies they developed for us as our heritage are still available for us today.

The sweat lodge is one of those ceremonies to help us find and maintain balance and harmony in our lives. It is a re-enactment of creation. It is a cycle of inner experience where broken and wounded human beings can go for healing. It takes our sensations back to the beginning.

It encourages an attitude of continual growth. It is designed to provide a safe place where we can concentrate on the spirits that come into the lodge to guide us on our quest for life. It directs our frame of reference of our thinking on the Earth Mother, which teaches us to understand the natural order that helps us to function in this life.

The Earth, our real mother, provides for all our physical needs. Nature is our greatest teacher and has within itself the blue prints for human behavior. When we pray and observe nature it teaches us to understand our place in the natural order of all things in the universe. The Earth Wisdom teaches us how we are to conduct ourselves.

The ancient wisdom of Mother Earth is contained within the rocks. When the heated rocks are placed in the lodge it re-enacts the process of growth. When we listen and watch, we receive messages that will assist us in our journey. It is a natural way that brings fire, water, air, earth and human beings together in a close association.

It produces a powerful physical and mental experience that brings us closer to the elemental forces of life. It helps us establish a connection to our culture and identity which helps nurture a healthy self-image as well as a sense of spiritual power. It builds a relationship that is both sacred and personal based on taking responsibility for becoming a fully awakened human being.

True power is found in the understanding that connects us to our innate wisdom and improves our clarity of thought and intent. It provides a time to seek answers, to state our intentions and to be reborn into the world with awareness and purpose.

The awareness wakes us to the understanding of what makes us different.

Unlike nature, we are designed with a free will and the ability to make choices and decisions. The results in our life are always determined by the choices and decisions we make…not by others. We are constantly implementing choices and decisions as our lives unfold.

Nature is designed with four parts of everything that is natural. There are four seasons, spring, summer, fall and winter. The wind has four directions, east, south, west and north. We human beings have four parts: legs, arms, body and head.

We each have four aspects, mental, physical, emotional and spiritual, which are all part of the circle of life, are interconnected and each have different functions. When any one of these aspects is out of balance, we do not function properly. If we have a physical problem it has a direct effect on our spirit, if our mental state is out of balance, it causes emotional turmoil.

When harmony and balance is lacking, sickness of various forms enter in its place.

This weakens the immune system. The spirit within needs to be in harmony and balance just as in all of creation. The greatest healing comes from ourselves because we want to be healed. We take responsibility for our own healing when we participate in our ceremonies.

Our traditional healing ceremonies restore balance to mind, body, emotion and spirit. This can include our daily offering of tobacco as well as the other ceremonies such as the sweat lodge, fasting, vision quest and the naming ceremony, which all help to restore our balance. When we start our healing journey we are making a commitment to ourselves, our families, and our community.

Although ceremonies are different from tribe to tribe, even from person to person, the basic beliefs are similar. We all want to take care of our spirit. Using sacred items such as the pipe, drum, and eagle feather, help us make the connection with creation.

All things of creation give us the teachings about love, kindness, caring, sharing, honesty and respect. When we pray, the spirits that travel with us hear our prayers, they recognize us clearly when we let them know our Spirit Name. It is said that through our Spirit Name is the way we begin moving toward our healing. It is how we know who we are, where we belong, where we are going and where we came from.

There are times when we get distracted from the powers we rely on, this happens when we get absorbed by negative feelings. Negative feelings such as: jealousy, anger, rage and resentments do more harm to us than the person or persons we direct them to. They block our spiritual growth because our own spirit gets caged up with those negative feelings.

The negative feelings have a direct effect on our physical, mental, emotional and spiritual health. Every time we say "I can't" or "I won't" we hold ourselves hostage.

The pain holds us back from becoming who we really are.

(Sweat Lodge 3 PP26)

Madoodiswan (The Sweat Lodge)

When a sweat is requested, the elder and his helpers go to prepare the lodge.

Tobacco, the first medicine herb, is offered to initiate the ceremony. Tobacco is offered for the wood, water and rocks that are gathered for the sweat. The fire keeper offers tobacco to the spirits of the four directions, mother earth and father sky as he prepares the fire pit.

(Sweat Lodge 3 PP29)

The fire keeper constructs a cradle to hold the rocks needed for the ceremony. The number of rocks depends on the type of sweat or the elder who runs the sweat. The rest of the wood is placed around the rocks and the fire is started.

The rocks are heated for several hours before the ceremony begins. Participants extend honor and respect to the Elder who runs the sweat. A lodge helper or fire keeper informs the participants of the nature of the ceremony. It might be a specific ceremony at someone's request or it may be a community sweat.

The fire keeper explains that the fire is sacred and nothing is to be thrown into it. He explains the sacred path from the fire to the lodge should not be crossed by anyone except the Elder. The Elder signals the fire keeper that the ceremony is about to begin.

The lodge is thoroughly cleaned with sage before the participants enter.

It is advisable for participants who are on any prescription medication that may be sensitive to heat to tell the Elder or the fire keeper. Each person is given an opportunity to offer tobacco to the sacred fire to acknowledge the grandfathers for their sacrifice. The lodge helper has sage for smudging before participants enter the lodge.

"Everyone get on your knees and crawl in clockwise." The fire keeper informs people the order in which they will enter. The fire keeper smudges everyone as they enter.

(Sweat Lodge 3 PP35)

When everyone is in the lodge, the Elder greets and informs everyone the nature of the sweat. He tells everyone if it becomes too difficult for anyone to acknowledge it, the door will be opened and that person can crawl out. If the person chooses to re-enter, it is done between rounds.

The Elder calls for the fire keeper to bring the hot rocks in, then asks for the door to be closed and starts the ceremony with prayers and songs. The number of rocks depends on the type of sweat. The unseen half of the circle moves to connect to the top half creating a full circle. As the Elder prays, he pours water on the hot rocks.

The lodge fills with a hissing sound and with hot steam or vapor.

There are usually four rounds of prayers. In the first round, the Elder prays to the spirits of all creation. The door is opened and fresh air enters. Participants can pray out loud or in silence, each focusing on different aspects and intent. Prayers can be for gratitude for all things of creation, for others, to honor the male and female principles, for self or for anything else the person wants to pray for.

Spirit energy moves in a clockwise direction when the Grandfather spirits are released. The lodge becomes a living entity when the power moves.

(Sweat Lodge 3 PP39)

We go in the sweat lodge to find balance and harmony for our mind, body and spirit and to learn from each other, because we want to stop the cycle of hurt and destruction so we can start: To heal ourselves; To heal our wounded relationships; To heal our families; To dry the tears of our children; To heal our communities; To heal our nation; To forgive the unforgivable. The hurt and destruction will stop here with me.

It is difficult to adequately describe what happens during a sweat. It is a personal journey and a personal experience. Each person experiences something uniquely different even though all share in the sweat. An individual needs to attend to have his or her own experience.

How the Sweat Lodge Came to the People (4)

March 2010, 42 slides

"Hello, my name is Big Wolf. I'm from the Bear Clan. Thank you for coming to listen, today we will be talking and learning about the sweat lodge."

(Sweat Lodge 4, PP04 - 05)

Mino-Bimaadiziwin (The Good Life)

A long time ago we lived a life of total submission to Gichi-Manidoo. (The Great Spirit) We did not have a written language. Ceremonies were our instructions about how to live and conduct ourselves. The Elders say, "If we do not do our ceremonies something else moves in."

The Mind Changer

A liquid called a "Mind changer" was brought to our land. Our way of life started to change as the people became obsessed with the liquid mind changer. The obsession of the liquid mind changer brought with it a lot of fighting, cheating, blaming, lying, stealing, jealousy, dishonesty, anger, fear and resentment.

The Little Boy and the Seven Grandfathers

One day a little boy began searching for ways to help his people because he could not stand all the ugliness and meanness that was around him.

He decided to go to the elders, if anybody would know what to do it would be them because they had been around the longest. After searching long and hard he found some elders who listened to him.

An elder woman says, "We've been waiting for you." An elder man says, "We will help. We will teach you."

The younger person says, "I will begin preparing." The elder says, "You will fast and seek your vision."

After fasting for a while the Oshkaabewis (spirit helper) came and took the boy past the moon and the star nations until they came to the lodge of the Seven Great Grandfathers.

The Grandfathers spoke their words directly to the mind of the little boy. "Look into the vessel. You were sent to take a special gift back to the people."

It was the Tree of Life. "The tree of life is the life of the people."

"This special gift is to be used to help the people become healthy again. You will remember every detail of how it is made and how the ceremony is to be conducted."

It took a long time for the Grandfathers to teach him all the instructions and when he returned to his people he was an old man.

The boy now, and old man says, "My people, I will explain the special gift the Seven Grandfathers sent."

"Place the sweat lodge in a location that will facilitate communication with the spirit world and build it with great care and respect to the environment to match its use. When we use it for ceremonial prayer, it provides the necessary ceremonial setting for spiritual connection, healing, purification, as well as fasting."

The sweat lodge ceremony follows the movement of the Medicine Wheel teachings.

It provides a gateway to a new beginning, uniting us to our spiritual journey. The sweat lodge ceremony is as intrinsic to the Medicine Wheel and honors and respects the earth as mother and the sky as father as well as the whole creation. The sweat lodge cleans our body, mind, spirit and emotions, and also renews our lives so we can get back the sacredness Gichi-Manidoo gave us.

The sweat lodge draws upon the four basic elements: earth, fire, water and air. It represents a womb where rebirth occurs. The people need a way to get back their traditional beliefs. The solution for the troubles the liquid mind changer brings to us is in utilizing this sacred gift the Seven Grandfathers gave us.

It draws out the poison of the liquid mind changer or any of the other substances.

It straightens out the behaviors that go along with the drunkenness. It repairs the damage we are doing to our spirit. It provides a place of refuge and a place to receive answers and guidance.

The Ceremony begins when a place is chosen for the sweat lodge. Start by digging two holes about 1 foot deep, 2 feet apart to the north, two to the east, two to the south, two to the west, a total of eight holes.

The Southern West pole represents the words and wisdom of the ancestors. The Northern West pole represents death and dreams of the past. The Western South pole represents words that have been spoken. The Eastern South pole represents words that will be spoken. The Western North pole represents old dreams. The Eastern North pole represents new dreams. The Southern East pole represents the word that needs to be spoken. The Northern East pole represents birth, rebirth and new beginnings.

Placing the poles in the ground symbolizes the role that Mother Earth plays in the healing, purifying and obtaining a spiritual experience. She is our first mother; she takes care of all our physical needs.

Four Spirit doors are aligned with the Four Sacred Directions. The human being uses only the eastern door. The two poles from the North and the two on the South are bent and tied together. This symbolically represents the connection between words and dreams. The two poles East and two on the West are bent together and tied symbolizing the continuity and harmony, and represent the continuous cycle of birth and rebirth. Connecting the East and West symbolizing the dreams of the ancestors, which are directly connected to the dreams of the future.

The door faces the direction of the rising sun, which symbolizes the rebirth of the participants that enter and emerge from the lodge. Four rings of willow are placed from bottom up and represent the four cycles of life and Creation. A pit is dug in the center of the lodge for the hot rocks (Grandfathers).

The sweat lodge is a full circle with both physical and spiritual aspects. The rings symbolize the four cycles of life as well as the four aspects of development.

The Sweat Lodge symbolizes the womb of Mother Earth. Grandmother watches over the lodge. The Lodge is covered with blankets or canvass. The door faces the direction of the rising sun. The earth from the pit is a place for the altar. The rocks are called grandfathers and are considered the wise ones, sometimes called the bones of Mother Earth.

When a request is made for a sweat, the preparation begins long before the participants arrive. Tobacco is offered by the fire keeper for the wood, rocks and water that are gathered for the ceremony. Tobacco is offered to the four directions, Father Sky, Mother Earth and placed in the fire pit. The wood is placed in the fire pit, then the Grandfathers are placed on the wood and the fire is started. There is a pail for the medicine water.

The Four Basic Elements, Fire, Water, Air and Earth are all present. Tobacco is offered to the Rocks, signifying we are related to them as we are related to all of creation. They are heated for several hours before the ceremony begins. The crescent shape symbolizes Grandmother Moon.

The lodge is thoroughly cleaned with sage before the participants enter.

The fire keeper informs everyone the order in which they will enter. The fire keeper smudges everyone as they enter and instructs, "Everyone get on your knees and crawl in clockwise."

When everyone is in the lodge, the Elder greets and informs everyone the nature of the sweat. He tells everyone if it becomes too difficult for anyone to acknowledge it, the door will be opened, the person can crawl out, and if the person chooses to re-enter, this is done between rounds.

The Elder calls for the fire keeper to bring the hot rocks in, then asks for the door to be closed and starts the ceremony with prayers and songs. The number of rocks depends on the type of sweat. The unseen half of the circle moves to connect to the top half creating a full circle. As the Elder prays, he pours water on the hot rocks. The lodge fills with a hissing sound and with hot steam or vapor.

We are introduced to the water spirit when the water is poured on the hot rocks. The water turns to steam, which represents the purifying and cleansing aspect of the water spirit. Although it's hot, the power of the water spirit purifies and cleanses us on a deeper level to support our healing process.

There are usually four rounds of prayers. The Elder begins the first round by praying to the spirits of all creation. The second round is for personal prayers concerning others and all of creation. The third round is for prayers for self. Participants can pray out loud or in silence, each focusing on different aspects and intent. Prayers can be for gratitude for all things of creation, for others, honor the male and female principles, for self or for anything else the person want to pray for.

Spirit energy moves in a clockwise direction when the grandfather spirits are released. The lodge becomes a living entity when the power moves.

The Sweat Lodge is used for centering, balancing, cleansing, healing, conducting important ceremonies, teaching our language and teaching the traditional ways of our people. Inside the lodge we support and encourage each other to endure to seek and find our connection to all that is sacred. This empowers us to sit in our power and speak our truth in a kind, gentle, compassionate, and loving manner that will continue to grow in our heart after the ceremony is complete.

The sweat lodge symbolizes the womb of Mother Earth and the turtle shell. It also symbolizes the interconnected system the Creator put in place when he finished creating the Earth and the Universe.

We use the sweat lodge to give thanks, to experience the power of renewal, to celebrate, to seek guidance and wisdom, or to mourn. After honoring the powers and energy of spirit, we leave the womb of Mother Earth a new person, leaving behind that which no longer serves us.

The mind, body, spirit purification process of the Sweat Lodge brings us to understand who we are. With such empowering understanding we start to reclaim our responsibility for and taking charge of our own spirit. We gain a new insight into our true path.

Medicine Wheel Teachings

Multiple Layers of Teachings (1)

October 2011, 46 slides

The teaching of the Medicine Wheel is Ancient Wisdom for Modern Times.

The Medicine Wheel is very subtle and rich in meaning. It is a mystical symbol and a living philosophy. It is a map to our innermost being.

The Medicine Wheel is not a belief system but a way to see life more clearly.

It teaches us how to find the good Red Road through life's many challenges.

The Medicine Wheel is adapted from our worldview of balance. First we notice that the Medicine Wheel is shaped like a circle. The circle is a vital element in our perspective, it has no beginning and no end, it is continuous and it includes all elements and all belong.

We consider the Medicine Wheel as a mental construct, because it orientates us to a time and space continuum. The Medicine Wheel divides our world into four different directions and applies specific meaning and significance to each direction.

This directional orientation is achieved simply by observing the natural world.

Regardless of where we are in life, there are four phases of the moon and typically four recognized seasons. These phases follow each other in sequential rotation; because of this, our personal Medicine Wheel is a reflection of our relationship to the natural evolution of the world. It serves as a way for us to focus and reconnect to the rhythm of the natural world.

The teachings of the Medicine Wheel are that everything comes from the same source of all existence, the Creator. From the Creator, all things come into existence and to the Creator all things return.

The Medicine Wheel is an ancient symbol for healing that initiates wholeness with self and oneness with all of life. The essence of the Medicine Wheel is about personal balance during movement, change and growth. When we are in-balance, we are in total alignment with ourselves', nature, and the universe.

Unfortunately, this alignment can be put out of balance if we are violated.

In our teachings, it is never healthy to be unbalanced with ourselves or to feel unbalanced by others, as we are all whole and equal in the eyes of the Creator.

The Medicine Wheel provides a visual representation of the concept of wellness that demonstrates the need for balance or well-rounded life. In order to maintain harmony and balance in our lives, we must pay attention to the four realms of wellness: the mental, physical, emotional and spiritual. To neglect or over-emphasize any of these four realms will result in an out-of-balance or out-of-round Medicine Wheel.

Imagine the Medicine wheel as a car with four tires, and each tire represents one of the four realms. If one or more tires are under inflated or over inflated, the Medicine Wheel/Car will be unbalanced. The road of life will be a bumpy one. We roll away through life more smoothly when our lives are well rounded or balanced.

We were given everything we need for our earth walk. The Creator put lessons everywhere in nature including a set of Principles, Laws and Values we are to live by. The key to the Medicine Wheel is movement, the way we move from one direction to another. We experience the nature of the directions with the intention of seeing the patterns of our own movement.

All the teachings of life are taught through the Medicine Wheel. This is where all of our ceremonies and traditional teachings come from.

The Principles, Laws and Values of the Medicine Wheel

There are multiple layers of teachings of the Medicine Wheel.

The Earth is an interconnected System. All life on Mother Earth and the Universe is interconnected.

The Basic Elements. The gifts of the Four Directions come in the form of Fire, Earth, Water and Air. To the East is Ishkode (Fire), to the South is Aki (Earth), to the West is Nibi (Water), and to the North is Noodin (Air or Wind).

(Multiple Teachings 1, PP20)

The Four Winds. Waabanong (East) symbolizes Beginning of Life, Zhaawanong (South) symbolizes Getting Along, Ningaabiiwanong (West) is about Getting Settled, and Giiwedinong (North) signifies Going Home.

The Four Great Powers of the Medicine Wheel are intelligences created by the Creator in order to bring the Universe into manifestation and keep it in being.

These Four Great Powers are "Spirit Beings" who express not so much the forces themselves but the intelligence of the directing mind that exercises those forces.

The Medicine Wheel shows us that the main capacity of these "Spirit Beings" is they are the caretakers of the Universe. They are represented on the Medicine Wheel as the four spokes of the four cardinal directions of the Universe. The directions are also known as the "Four Winds".

The Spirit of the East is the power of illumination that opens the spiritual eye and brings enlightenment and understanding. This is the power of new beginnings and a new fresh life. The color of the Spirit of the East is Yellow, the color of the rising sun and of illumination.

The Spirit of the South is the power of life. The south is the sun at its highest point, it's the direction from which warm winds blow. It represents trust, sensitivity, love, nourishment and peace. The color of the Spirit of the South is Red.

The Spirit of the West is the power of strength and introspection.

It is the power of growth, which enables realization to develop. It is the power of growth to full maturity and the power of self-examination. The color of the Spirit of the West is Black, the color of formlessness from which all forms comes.

The Spirit of the North is the power of renewal and of the quickening of the Spirit. It is the power of winter, when nothing appears to be growing, but Mother Earth is gathering her energies for springtime to come. It is the power of concentration and clarity of intent. The color of the Spirit of the North is White, regarded as the color of perfection because it is the sum of all the colors.

The North represents knowledge around "how" and the wisdom of "why."

When we sit in the north, we contemplate the question of "Why am I here?"

In the East we experience enlightenment about ourselves by asking the question "Where am I going?"

Our quest to the South stimulates us to examine our own identity and to get rid of the garbage we have been carrying around.

To the West we ask, "Where did I come from?" There we learn to look inward and accept the changes as a process of new beginnings.

At the center we complete our journey around and through the circle. Our medicine path leads us to this clearing where we sit and consider our future as we think about what we have learned and integrated.

The Four Basic Elements are to the east Fire, to the south Earth, to the west Water, and Air is in the north.

Guardians of the Four Elements. To the East is Grandfather Sun, Mother Earth to the South, to the West is Grandmother Moon, and to the North is Father Sky, our First Family.

(Multiple Teachings 1, PP31)

The Seven Sacred Directions

In addition to the Four Winds, we add above Father Sky, which is about understanding, spiritual awareness, detachment and seeing the bigger picture.

Mother Earth, below, is about the unseen and the unconscious. It's about taking care of self, of looking beneath the surface.

The Center or within is Truth. It is our true self, our core. It is the deepest aspect of our spiritual self.

The Center of the Medicine Wheel is where the meaning of the teachings comes from. When we look at the Medicine Wheel, we start from the Self, and as we look outwards, we make our Circle. This is how the teachings of the Medicine Wheel represent the journey of the people.

Spirituality means waking up and learning all the lessons the school of life is teaching us. Everything that happens to us is a lesson. Most of us have been sleep walking through life, living superficially on the surface of life unaware of the miracles, the beauty of our wonder-filled earth.

Spirituality means waking up to the miracles of our own existence, and also to the beauty, wonder, majesty and splendor of our own life.

Spirituality means waking up to the sacredness within each of us and bringing out that sacredness in our creativity, skills, talents and strength…our gifts of life. It means waking up to our possibilities and capabilities even though we may not be aware of them at the moment.

It means waking up and accepting the challenges to change the way we think, the way we live our lives and the way we perceive things. It means waking up and being willing to learn something about ourselves, about others, the earth, and about the Creator.

It means waking up to the reverence for all of life realizing that we are but one strand of the web of life. It means waking up and becoming aware that as long as we are still breathing there is more that is right with us than wrong with us.

The Cycle of Seasons. Ziigwan (Spring), Niibin (Summer), Dagwaagin (Fall) and Biboon (Winter).

The Four Sacred Colors. Ozaawaa (Yellow), Miskwaa (Red), Makadewaa (Black), and Waabishkaa (White).

The Four Colors of the Medicine Wheel also teaches us that the four symbolic races are all part of the same human family. We are all brothers and sisters living on the same Mother Earth.

The Cycle of Life. Abinoojiinh (Baby), Oshki-aya'aa (Youth), Gichi-aya'aa (Adult), and Gete-aya'aa (Elder).

We move from the East on the Circle of Life to the South, to the West and to the North, combining the gifts of the Four Directions, Mind, Heart, Body and Spirit, we come full circle in our development.

The Four Aspects of Development. Enendimowin (Mental), Enamanijoon (Emotional), Wiiyow (Physical), and Jiibik (Spiritual).

Animals Associated with the Four Directions. Migizi (Eagle) to the East, Ma'iingan (Wolf) to the South, Makwa (Bear) is to the West, and Mashkode Bizhiki (Bison) is to the North.

The journey we embarked on today is not complete by a single revolution of the Medicine Wheel, it is only a new beginning. Having reached the place we are now, our journey has just begun. We must now decide whether we want to go forward further and deeper.

(Multiple Teachings 1, 46)

The Circle of Life (2)

September 2013, 46 slides

(Cycle of Life PowePoint slides)
We find Wisdom in the Circle of Life.

The Circle

The Circle is the first design of Creation. It is an object of nature. It is a symbol by which we understand and describe our world. It is the heart of our value system. The Circle is the foundation of our spirituality and the heart of our family structure.

Our Worldview

The Circle of Life is the basic principle in our worldview that is comprehensive and spiritual in nature. Everything within the Circle has a purpose, where all things and beings depend on one another for survival.

We live in an interconnected, interrelated and interdependent system.

When we enlarge our view of the world, it helps us to understand our life and our place in creation much better.

The universe works like a hall of mirrors, how we see our world depends on our frame of reference. Our ceremonies teach us to put our frame of reference of our thinking on the Earth Mother and the Universe.

My culture operates in a "CIRCULAR" way of seeing life. It allows us to see the sacred forms of circles everywhere. Spiritual energy flows in circles. Forms and circles are the most obvious representations of the Universe.

We are not oriented to operate in a *linear* way. Spiritual energy does not move in a line.

Traditional Teachings were given to the ancestors at the beginning of time. They are relevant today. They connect us to natural and spiritual worlds. It is a Creation-based form of spirituality that has at its center the symbol of the Sacred Circle.

The Medicine Wheel

Symbols are the oldest, most sacred language. The Medicine Wheel is a symbol that helps us understand and share spiritual concepts, principles, and truths - all things related to life, the Great Cycle of Life.

A Medicine Wheel is a teaching circle that explains that everything grows as a system of circles and cycles. Understanding the significance of the Sacred Circle is the first step towards understanding the Medicine Wheel.

The Medicine Wheel is an adaption of our worldview. It contains multiple layers of teachings. It contains all we need to live and conduct our lives in a good way.

Bawaajigewin (Dream/Vision) Creation Story

The Order of Creation

Starting in the East and going clockwise, the Creator first made Minerals, then Plants to the south, next came Animals to the West, and finally Humans to the north.

The mineral world is the first order of creation. It too is on the Medicine Wheel. In the east we have rocks, followed by gravel in the south, sand in the west, and gems to the north.

The plant world is the second order of creation. Trees are in the East, Grasses in the South, Flowers to the West, and Herbs at the North.

The Animal world is the third order of creation. The Four legged are in the East, the Winged ones to the South, Swimmers are in the West, and Crawlers in the North.

The Four Sacred Colors of the Human family are the last order of creation. Yellow in the East, Red to the South, Black to the West and White to the North.

The Four Basic Elements, Fire, Water, Earth, and Air are the building blocks of all creation.

The Seven Sacred Directions are Anishinaabe Ishinaamowim, (the Anishinaabe Worldview). It starts with the four directions, Father Sky above, Mother Earth below, and at the Center, the Self.

There are Four Seasons starting in the East, Spring, Summer, Fall, and Winter. The Four Sacred Colors of the human family are Yellow, Red, Black, and White. The Cycle of Life starts with Baby, then Youth, Adult, and Elder.

The direction of growth of the Four Aspects of Self is, Spiritual, Physical, Emotional, and Mental. The Four Directions of Healing are first Individual, followed by Family, then Community, then Nation.

We humans are made of these four basic elements; Spirit/Fire in the East, Blood/Water to the South, Body/Earth to the West, and Breath/Air to the North. If an element is broken down we see a direct connection to an aspect of our life.

The Cycle of Life again is Baby, Youth, Adult, and Elder. Knowing and remembering our place in the Cycle of Life helps us feel the deep connection to our true nature. We grow and change like the seasons. Each stage of life goes through a Springtime, Summertime, Autumn time, and Wintertime.

The four validations for our inherent needs are Recognition/for the special person we are; Attention/to nurture the child within; Affection/to heal our wounds; and Approval/for who we are.

Our earth walk is divided between two hemispheres. Upper hemisphere, sky dome, symbolizes our spiritual aspect. Lower hemisphere is the physical environment, the horizontal line represents the path of events, and our Earth walk is at center.

Principles, Laws and Values

We understand the principles, laws and values that were given to Creation.

If we live in harmony with these, we experience harmony, balance, and peace. If we live out of harmony with these, we experience chaos, frustration, and stress.

The Seven Grandfather Teachings. To adhere to these teachings is to be guided by these values. Migizi (Eagle)/Zaa-gi-idwin (Love) is at the Center of the Wheel. Above is Amik (Beaver)/Nbwa-kaa-win (wisdom), at the bottom is Mikinaak (Turtle)/Deb-we-win (Truth). On the right upper Makwa (Bear)/Aak-wade'ewin (Bravery), at the lower right is Ma'iingan (Wolf)/Dbaa-deni-ziwin Humility, at upper left Mashkode Bizhiki (Buffalo)/Mnaa-dendi-mowin (Respect), and the lower left is Masaba (Bigfoot)/Gwek-waado-zwin (Honesty). This leads to Mino-Bimadaadiziwin (The Good Life).

The Four Gifts. The Yellow Nation was given the gift of Fire, the Red Nation was given the gift of Earth, the Black Nation's gift is Water, and White Nation's gift is Air.

The Four Sacred Elements Help All of Life to Exist.

The Guardians of the Four Elements

To the East and Fire is Grandfather Sun who has the power of heat and light. The Guardian to the South and Earth is Mother Earth who has the power of growth and healing. The West Guardian of Water is Grandmother Moon who has the power to purify and of renewal. The Guardian for the North and Air is Father Sky who has the power of the breath of life.

The Balanced Way of using our Energy is Determine, Hold, Give, and Receive. This is aligning with the Universal Rhythm.

The Imbalanced Way of Using Energy is the opposite, Receive, Give, Hold, and Determine. Problems often arise with this type of energy use creating imbalances and disharmony.

Each of us is given a place on the Medicine Wheel at the time of our birth. We're born into the rhythm of our Earth Mother. That becomes our first perception of our physical world.

We go around the Medicine Wheel Many Times in our Quest for Wholeness. In order to achieve wholeness we move around the Wheel to see life from different perspectives. Each revolution brings more clarity than the one before, as different aspects of our being are revealed through the lessons we learn. When we step into the Circle, we align our self to the rhythm of our Earth Mother, the Universe and with Nature that constantly reminds us of movement through the changing of the seasons.

The Gift of the Five Senses on the Medicine Wheel, Sight is in center, to the east Touch, south is Hearing, Taste is to the west and Smell to the north. The Five Senses helps us relate to and survive in the physical world.

Ni-taw-Wi-Gi-Iwe-win. (Rites of Passage) Our Rites of passage start with Trust and moving clockwise, Autonomy, Initiative, Accomplishment, Identity, Intimacy, Generosity, and Integrity. Each stage of feeling must be completed to move toward maturity.

The Four Parts of Self or State of Being

We were given the gift of Being, named for the four parts of our human existence, Spiritual, Emotional, Physical and Mental. We are called Anishinaabe. We are to try and keep these four parts in balance as best we can to function as Anishinaabeg.

Our Spiritual Self

Our Spiritual aspect is our inner essence, our soul. It's the part that exists beyond time and space, which connects us to the Universal Source and to the oneness of life.

It is our spiritual existence that allows us to experience a feeling of belonging in the universe, and gives us a deeper meaning and purpose. Our Spiritual aspect provides a foundation for the development of the other aspects.

Our Emotional Self

Our Emotional aspect gives us the ability to experience life deeply and to relate to one another and the world on a feeling level. It is the part of us that seeks meaningful contact and connection with others. It is the part that allows us to feel a full range of our human existence with our five senses.

Our Physical Self

Our Physical aspect is our body, which includes our ability to survive in the material world, including learning how to take good care of it. It also means developing skills to live comfortably and effectively in the World.

Our Mental Self

Our Mental aspect is our intellect, our ability to think and reason. It can be our greatest gift and at times our greatest curse, it can cause us terrible confusion or bring us profound understanding. Developing our mental aspect allows us to be able to think clearly and be open-minded.

All four aspects of our being are equally important. To feel whole and lead a healthy and satisfying life we need to spend time understanding, developing, healing and integrating each aspect. We were created and intended to be human.

Mino-Bimaadiziwin (The Good Life)

We were given everything we need to make our earth-walk at the time of creation.

Each of us was given the gift of Mino-bimaadiziwin.

The basic principle of life is not to get to the end of the Red Road, but to enjoy the journey.

Lessons of the Four Directions (3)

January 2014, 28 slides

(4 Directions PowerPoint Slides)

Ceremonies are our First Duty

When we engage in our ceremonies, we awaken and affirm our innate wisdom. We invoke our ability to heal mind, body, heart and spirit. We connect with Nature and our own natural rhythm.

The Cycle of Life. Life is a gift, and to honor that gift, we were given tobacco.

The Four Basic Elements, starting in the east, are fire, water, earth, and air. They are essential elements to everything in creation.

The Circle of Life moves from Baby, to Youth, Adult, and Elder. All living things have a moment in which they become "alive" which marks the beginning point on the circle of life. Life is a path, on which we are invited by the Creator to grow and develop in all areas of our lives.

The Cycle of Life is structured around the clan system. For Red Lake Nation, the Eagle is at the center, to the east is Turtle, to the south Otter, west is Bear, north is Bullhead, above is Pine Marten, and below is Kingfisher.

The Cycle of Life. We are all born into the rhythm of Mother Earth. We are intended and created to be human. Our journey begins when the Creator breathes the spirit of life into us, a spirit that motivates all life in the great circle.

Our spirit enters our physical body at the time of birth and we enter the world from the direction in the East.

We are a spirit having a human experience. We learn to walk the wheel of life in time with the rhythms of Mother Earth to discover who we are and to find our purpose in life.

The cycle of life symbolizes the natural cycles of birth, growth, death and regeneration. Traditionally a child's first teaching is of the four directions of the medicine wheel.

The Rhythm and Heartbeat of Mother Earth is the Drum.

We are each given a place on the Medicine Wheel at the time of birth. Imagine the Medicine Wheel as a clock. January is at 12 o'clock, followed clockwise by the remaining months. The month of your birth is where you are on the Medicine Wheel.

The Four States of Being are, starting in the east, spiritual, emotional, physical, and mental.

Our life consists of four aspects or levels of being. Each person is responsible to maintain balance of these four aspects. In order to have balance, wholeness and fulfillment, we need to develop and integrate all four of these aspects within ourselves.

Each person is responsible to maintain a healthy balance of these four aspects. Neglecting one aspect leads to an imbalance of the whole self.

Our traditional teachings encompass all aspects of our lives. The teachings are about the inseparability of the four aspects of our being.

The medicine wheel is an interconnected system of teachings that speak of the need for balance, harmony and respect. Balance, harmony and respect are maintained through the interdependency of the forces.

The Four Colors of the Medicine Wheel

In the east is Yellow/baby/spring, south symbolizes Red/youth/summer, west represents Black/adult/Fall, and north is White/Elder/Winter. Each color is a spirit that is associated to a life stage. If you were born in a particular season you will be more influenced by that color's spirit.

The Cycle of Life

We are all born into the rhythm of Mother Earth. We are intended and created to be human. Our spirit enters our physical body at the time of birth and we enter the world from the direction in the East. Life is a path by which we are invited by the Creator to grow and develop in all aspects of our life.

Everybody needs a balanced life. Finding balance and harmony helps an individual to live the good life.

Spiritual Aspect

This is our inner essence, the part of us that exists beyond space and time. It connects us with the universal source and the oneness of all life. Developing our awareness of our spiritual self allows us to experience a feeling of belonging with a deeper purpose and meaning in our life. Our spiritual level provides the foundation for the development of the other levels.

Emotional Aspect

This gives us the ability to experience life on a deeper level so we can relate to one another and with the world on a feeling level. It's the part of us that seeks meaningful contact and connection with others. Developing our emotional level allows us to feel the full range of the human experience through our five senses and find fulfillment in our relationships with our self and with others.

Physical Aspect

This is our physical body, which includes our ability to survive and thrive in the Material world. Developing our physical level involves learning to take good care of our body. It means developing skills to live comfortably and effectively in the world.

Mental Aspect

This is our intellect, our ability to think and reason. It consists of our thoughts, attitudes, beliefs and values. It can be our greatest gift and at times it can be our greatest curse. Developing our mental level allows us to think clearly and be open-minded. Our mind enables us to gather information, knowledge and wisdom from our life experiences and from the world around us.

The Five Senses: At the center is sight, followed by smell in the east, taste in the south, touch in the west, and hearing in the north.

The Seven Grandfathers Teachings. At the center is Wisdom, to the east is Love, to the south Respect, to the west Bravery, to the north Honesty, Humility is above and below is Truth.

The Four Directions of Growth. To the east is Spirit & Spiritual Insight, to the south are Emotions & Feelings, to the west is the Body & Physical motion, and to the north are Mind Thoughts & Attitudes.

The Medicine Wheel Teachings Help us Find: to the east we will find a strong inner spirit; to the south, inner peace; to the west we find a Strong healthy body; and to the north we find a healthy mind.

The Eight Stages or Feelings that must be successfully completed: This is the path we travel through life. Each stage represents a time in our life. Trust, autonomy, initiative, accomplishment, identity, intimacy, generosity, integrity.

We would traditionally experience the "rites of passage" ceremony at each stage to mark our transition into a new way of being. If these transitions do not occur, we will feel incomplete on some level.

The Creator put lessons everywhere in Nature. We are taught to place our frame of reference of our thinking on our Earth Mother. We are taught to think in circles. We use Nature to better understand ourselves, and our association with others.

We grow, we change like the seasons. We learn from each direction as we grow through each of the directions of the Medicine Wheel.

Medicine Wheel Introduction I (4)

April 2014, 17 slides

The Medicine Wheel is a circle Divided by a cross or an X that creates the four Directions.

Our ancestors used the tools from the environment - also called Mother Earth - for hundreds of years to teach lessons about life. The tools helped our Ancestors pass on important teachings and information based on the Seven Directions of the Medicine Wheel.

All the teachings about life are contained in the ancient symbol of the Medicine Wheel.

The Medicine wheel is a tool that teaches us about the many gifts of the Creator. It is a Sacred Circle that teaches about balance and makes harmony meaningful.

The Medicine Wheel provides a holistic foundation upon which we can base our lives. All the teachings about life are contained in the ancient symbol of the Medicine Wheel.

Medicine Wheel Teachings

This Sacred Knowledge was given to us to make our walk on Mother Earth. The teachings have been followed and shared for generation after generation. We honor the ones that walked before us for they are the ones that sat in sacred circles many times with the hope that we their children and grandchildren will follow in their path.

The Seven Sacred Directions. Each direction is represented by a color. Yellow represents east, red south, black west, and white north. Blue represents Father Sky, Green Mother Earth, and Purple represents the center or self. As we journey through life we encounter each of these directions in our mental, physical, emotional, and spiritual growth.

The Four Cardinal Directions on the Medicine Wheel are the Four Sacred Directions. Yellow represents east and the Yellow Race, Red south and the Red Race, Black west and the Black Race, and White north and the White Race. These are the four basic colors we use on the Medicine Wheel. Each color is unique and has significant meaning.

Each direction constitutes a path of self-realization and self-reflection, which leads to the very core of our being.

The Four Basic Elements. Each direction represents an element. East represents fire; south represents earth; west water; and north air.

Each direction is represented by a season as well, east for Spring, south for Summer, west for Autumn, and north for Winter.

Seven Grandfather Teachings.

The teachings begin in the northern direction and move down to the center.

Wisdom, Truth, and Bravery are at the center. Love is to the East, Respect at the South, Honesty to the West, and Humility to the North. The directions remind us of the need for balance in the world and the balance we must strive for everyday within ourselves.

The Medicine Wheel can be used to better understand ourselves and the world around us. It is an insightful tool that offers us to see the big picture and how our choices and actions impact our lives and the world around us.

Life revolves around the Circle of Life. The Circle of Life is the basic principle of our worldview. Everything within the circle has a purpose.

Each of us will go around the Medicine Wheel many times during our lifetime.

Introduction to the Medicine Wheel II (5)

April 2014, 20 slides

The Circle is the First Design of Creation

Understanding the significance of the Circle is the first step towards understanding the Medicine Wheel. Our Traditional beliefs are a creation-based form of spirituality that has at the center the symbol of the Sacred Circle.

Everything is a Circle or Cycle. The Circle is an object of Nature, a symbol or a framework by which we understand and describe our world.

The Circle of Life is the basic principle of our worldview. Our worldview is comprehensive and spiritual in nature. Everything in Nature expresses itself in circular patterns.

The Circle is fundamental to our philosophy; everything in Life resembles the Circle and represents the togetherness of the people. One of the fundamental teachings of the Circle is that it expresses a participatory philosophy in which we are a part of the natural world.

Our Ancestors have always engaged in ceremonies and rituals to honor life that invoked the powers that dwelled within to connect to Nature, and the

Earth Mother, to bring them into alignment with harmony and balance.

Since we didn't have a written language long ago, we were given ceremonies and sacred symbols, which are all contained in the Medicine Wheel. They thrived on symbolism and saw the world in terms of circles and cycles.

Like them we too can use this framework of symbolism to incorporate the circular and spiral energies.

Symbolism is the most powerful language we were given so we can understand and communicate with spiritual concepts and truths. The ancient symbol of the Medicine Wheel represents and expresses meaning, and meaning provides us with the purpose and understanding.

The Medicine Wheel teachings were originally explained orally by drawing a circle on the ground with gradual overlaying symbols as an Elder explained meaning.

The Medicine Wheel is central to all living things. Everything has a symbolic meaning, purpose and a function.

The basic aspect of the Medicine Wheel is the Circle, which defines the order of the world and the cycle of all life. The Circle is symbolic of the never-ending cycle of life that has no beginning and no ending. It is all-inclusive rather than exclusive, and brings things together rather than separating them.

The Medicine Wheel symbolizes the individual journey we must each take to find our own path. The teachings are philosophies of life. The teachings give us a way of looking at, and making sense of the world as well as help us find our way through life.

The Medicine Wheel teachings are among the oldest teachings, which are anchored to the Seven Directions. The teachings serve as a reminder of our place in the world. The teachings remind us how we are to live our lives.

The Medicine Wheel has many meanings on various levels. There are multiple teachings of the Medicine Wheel. The grains of sand on a beach would never equal the number of teachings contained within the mysteries of the Medicine Wheel.

The Circle or Wheel is a representative of the Creator or the Universe, as well as one's own personal space or personal universe. The Medicine Wheel in its simplest form is a symbol we use to interpret and describe the world in which we live. It represents harmony, connection and a symbol of peaceful interaction among all living things on earth.

The Medicine Wheel is an introspection tool that is a nonlinear model for human development. It helps us to redirect our thinking away from the linear way of thinking. It helps us deepen our understanding by encouraging participation. It represents humanity, diversity, unity, inclusion and healing.

The Medicine Wheel is a symbol for living as human beings and helps us as human beings to understand how to live a healthy life. All parts of the Medicine wheel are important and depend on each other in the Circle of Life. What affects one affects all, for this reason it teaches that harmony, balance and respect for all parts of life is needed to sustain life.

The Medicine Wheel is the fundamental center of our worldview and spirituality, which teaches us about our place in the universe and our relationship to all of creation. The Medicine Wheel in its simplest form is a symbol we use to interpret and describe the world in which we live. It represents harmony, connection and a symbol of peaceful interaction among all living things on earth.

Numbers have always played an important role in our culture, because many aspects in Nature are expressed in fours. The Medicine Wheel is round to represent the Circle of Life. The spokes that cross at the center represent how all things in the natural world come in fours.

Movement on the Medicine wheel, like our ceremonies, is clock-wise or in a sun-wise direction which aligns with the forces of Nature. It is a balanced system, yet embraces movement and change like the cycles of Nature. It helps us to connect with Nature and our natural rhythm, which puts us into a state of harmony.

The Medicine Wheel is a powerful ancient symbol of the Earth, and the Universe. It's a spiritual tool that contains all the teachings of the Earth and the Universe. It's a teachings circle and a balanced, polarity system and a symbol of harmony. It teaches the reality of conflict and struggle. It is a physical manifestation of spiritual energy, and a window in which we can see clearly what is going on within us.

The Medicine Wheel is a silent teacher that guides us through the circle of lessons we must pass through in order to complete our life journey. We can use the Ancient Symbol of the Medicine Wheel and its Teachings to develop our personal life if we decide to put forth the effort to change our lives.

   We are once again at a time, when we are invited to revisit the time-honored teachings, to embrace the old ways, so we can renew our lost connection to the Sacred Teachings. As Anishinaabeg we are coded for ceremonies and rituals, it is in our "DNA" from our ancestors. When we start engaging in our ceremonies, we will reawaken and reaffirm our innate wisdom and our power to invoke our ability within to heal our body, mind and spirit.

PowerPoint Teachings
Last Teachings

Anishinaabemowin (1)

November 2013, 17 slides

   Note: I attended Larry's last four teachings and wrote stories about them as part of the work I do with the tribe. All the words of the PowerPoint teachings are contained within the stories in addition to Larry's aside comments.

Written by me December 20, 2013

Culture/Language Revitalization Event Held at Red Lake Middle School
November 20, 2013

Darkness falls early in late November on the Red Lake Indian Reservation. It is near biboon (winter), a time for teaching and learning. A steady stream of headlights slowly came to a halt in neat little rows at the middle school parking lot around 5:30 p.m. Always seeming like a long walk from the lot to entryway, guests passed through two sets of doors before being greeted by a friendly security guard who politely requested all to sign in.

The language and cultural event was originally scheduled for the middle school mini-theater. But upon entering, visitors were greeted by a cheerful middle school principle, Susan Ninham. She directed all to the right, explaining the venue had changed to the school's more appropriate "Culture Room."

While a few entered the culture room, most walked to the high school cafeteria where a traditional wild rice hot dish graced the menu. Slowly the room began to fill. Eyes wandered about the circular, colorful, and rustic room. A variety of seating was available, half-log furniture, tables, benches and chairs. High on the walls were sculptures depicting Red Lake's seven major clans. Below each symbol was the name of the clan written in Ojibwemowin; Makwa (Bear) Mikinaak (Turtle), Awaazisii (Bullhead), Waabizheshi (Marten), Migizi (Eagle), Ojiig (Fisher), and Ogiishkimanisii (Kingfisher).

An estimated 75 people from Red Lake, Leech Lake, and even a non-Indian or two, rose as Mike Smith, Sr. (Leech Lake) offered the invocation.

Below Mikinaak, a cartoon-like image of an elder wrapped in a blanket and smoking a pipe, was cast on a screen with the words; "Boozhoo, miigwech wii gaa kaan dazo yaag." (Hello, thank you for striving to learn.) Violet Stillday, the wife of the evening's tutor, posted the screen image, the first of a Power Point presentation.

To the right of the screen stood her husband, spiritual advisor and teacher, Gichi-Ma'iingan (Larry Stillday), who commented on how appropriate it was to have this teaching surrounded by the clan symbols.

"Never use the word loss," Stillday began, "we have lost nothing. We stopped using it! Language is essential to preserving our culture. Hopefully we take it up again. It's still here because our land is still here. This is where the Creator put it, on the land. Our ancestors are waiting for us."

The Lessons of the Medicine Wheel

Chi-Ma'iingan would combine the cultural lessons of the Medicine Wheel with Ojibwemowin. The PowerPoint slides would illustrate his subject.

"The teachings of our ancestors are still relevant for us today," said Stillday. "Migizi, (bald eagle) is our teacher for balance and harmony. As Anishinaabeg, we were given a way to think, see and speak. We are not oriented to think in a "linear way" as we do today. We were originally oriented to think and operate in a "circular way" of relating and looking at life. This is the deeper meaning of "Indian time."

"Our language and culture go hand in hand. Gichi-Manidoo (the Creator) put in place a set of principles, laws, and values for all life forms to abide by. Anything that has life must abide by these principles," said Stillday.

"We are all at different places in the Circle of Life," he went on. "Imagine the wheel with 12 spokes, each spoke represents the month/date of our birth. That's where we are on the Medicine Wheel. We go around the Wheel, the Creator has invited us to walk the Wheel, to walk this path of life."

He then went on to explain the quadrants of the Medicine Wheel and how, though simple, contains many teachings. He illustrated his words with a series of slides, always beginning in the East, then moving clockwise to the South, West, and finally North.

First he explained the four **Sacred Elements of Life**. In the East we find Ishkode, (fire), then Nibi (water) to the South, Aki (earth), to the West, and Noodin (air/wind) at the North. "All life forms consist of these four elements," said Stillday.

Next came the four **Sacred Directions**, Waabanong (east), Zhaawanong (south), Ningaabiiwanong (west), and Giiwedin (north), which were followed by the four **Sacred Seasons**, Ziigwan (spring), Niibin (summer), Dagwaagin (fall), and Biboon (winter). "We all grow and change like the seasons," said Stillday.

The Four **Sacred Colors** or the colors of the human race followed; Ozaawaa (yellow), Miskwaa (red), Makadewaa (black), and Waabishkaa (white). "I often hear the word 'they' when people speak of the colors," observed Stillday. "We have lots of friends who are half-white. We need to quit saying, 'they,' it's not about Indians, it's about people."

Stillday went on. "The basis of all our teachings is Bimaadiziwin - the Circle of Life," he said. "This too is on the wheel. We start the Circle of Life as an Abinoojiiyens, (baby) and then we grow to Oshkiniigii (youth), followed by Gichi-aya'aa (adult), and finally Gete-aya'aa (elder)."

"Finally we have the **Four Aspects of Self**; Manidoowaadiziwin (spiritual), inamanji'owin (emotional), niiyaw (physical), and inaandamowin (mental). Our language is still here on the land, it just needs to be picked up," he said.

Niizhwaaso Mishoomis Gikinoo'amaagewwinnaan

(The Teachings of the Seven Grandfathers)

The Circle on the screen now appeared as a sphere or in 3-D as it gets more complex, now showing the seven directions rather than four.

"Our language and our teachings are anchored in the **Seven Sacred Directions**," Stillday went on. "We start with four mentioned before, Waabanong (east), Zhaawanong (south), Ningaabiiwanong (west), and Giiwedin (north). Above is Ishpeming (Father Sky), below is Gidakiminoon (Mother Earth) and then Naawayi'ii (center or self)."

"The **Seven Teachings** have long been part of our language. Gichi-Manidoo gave us a way to think and live," Stillday explained, "and they too are on the Medicine Wheel. To the East is Nibwaakaawin (wisdom), to the South is Minwaadendamowin (respect), to the West is Aakodewewin (bravery/courage), to the North Gwekowaadiziwin (honesty), above is Debwewin (truth), below is Dibaadendiziwin (humility), and at the center is Zaagi'idiwin (love). These are the principles that we need to live by."

"Everything in life is interconnected, interrelated and interdependent on another. This system cannot be changed," declared Stillday. "When we have a detachment from the system, what we say and what we do affects that system. The hurt of one is the hurt of all. If we see drunks, we don't walk away, because these are all good people."

"As we learn of these things, people will wake up. We will hear something and we say, 'it seems like I knew that;' that, 'aha!' moment. It is something deep inside all of us. When a person realizes that, 'I don't know…that I don't know,' then we can begin. We realize then that, 'now I know…that I don't know'. We are saying in effect, 'I'm open to the message'. Our grandpa and grandma lived like that."

"Why? What happened? We don't know," said Stillday. "But quit teaching that we have lost something, we haven't lost anything! These are our teachings! These are our ceremonies! We still have these ceremonies. Where do we start? We need to start like a child. Our ancestors knew every part of the development of a child and had rites of passage ceremonies."

"In a child's first ceremony, he or she is given a name. The naming ceremony comes from actions at the beginning of time. It goes back to our creation story where Ma'iingan (Wolf), then a companion of Anishinaabe (Original Man), named all things on earth, gave everything an Ojibwe name," said Stillday. "Therefore our language is in nature. Why? So we can live! So honor that child. Help he or she realize that; 'I've accomplished something, I am someone.'"

"This first teaching is an introduction. It is to help you think about…what you are thinking about," said a smiling Stillday. "We change, culture changes, but the teachings remain the same."

Language Summit Presentation (2)

December 2013, 19 slides

Story Written January 11, 2014

Miskwaagamiiwi'zaaga'iganing Gichi-Ojibwemowin Maawanji'idwin

(Red Lake Ojibwe Language Summit)

Held at Seven Clans Event Center

The Language Summit held at Seven Clans Casino on December 18, 2013, was only the most recent of many happenings Red Lake Anishinaabeg are pursuing in order to revitalize Ojibwemowin and the culture of the land. Among the keynote speakers was Larry Stillday.

A chilly Monday evening would not deter some 200 people from gathering at the Seven Clans Event Center to attend a community celebration and feast. The gathering would mark the onset of the Miskwaagamiiwi'zaaga'iganing Gichi-Ojibwemowin Maawanji'idwin. (Red Lake Ojibwe Language Summit)

The event drew many first and other fluent speakers, elders, and scores of others interested in various aspects of Ojibwemowin revitalization. Most came from Red Lake, but many came from other tribes and/or communities.

Larry would use the opportunity to present some of his basic teachings regarding the importance of language to Ojibwe culture and overall health and healing, and some basic teachings on the Medicine Wheel using more Ojibwemowin in the PowerPoint presentation than usual.

Keynote: Gichi-Ma'iingan (Larry Stillday)

Stillday uses a PowerPoint presentation to illustrate the teachings and many layers of the Medicine Wheel. "Thank you for coming to listen to this," Stillday began.

"Ojibwemowin, this is the language we've been given," said Stillday. Let's begin by picking back up our language."

"This is the way our language was put into place. The Great Spirit made everything in creation to always grow as a system of circles and cycles. Anything that has life always follows a circular and cyclic principle," said Stillday.

"Our language and culture go hand in hand. The Creator made everything in creation to always grow as a system of circles and cycles," he said. "Gichi-Manidoo (the Creator) put in place a set of principles, laws and values for all life forms to live by and to guide our earth journey. Anything that has

life must abide by these principles. Gichi-Manidoo put those lessons everywhere in nature."

"Gidishkoniganina (Red Lake Nation) is also on the Medicine Wheel," noted Stillday. "Our Four Districts start in the East with Maadaabiimong (Redby), to the South is Ogaakaaning, (Red Lake), to the West is Gaa-asini-isikaag (Little Rock), and to the North is Obaashiing (Ponemah) which are all part of Miskwaagamiiwizaaga'iganiing (The Red Lake Reservation and Lake)".

"Our language comes from actions at the beginning of time," Chi-Ma'iingan went on. "It goes back to our creation story where Nanabozho and Ma'iingan, then companions, put our language in nature by naming everything on earth, giving everything an Ojibwe name. Therefore our language is in nature. Our language is there, and it is still alive. Our language is very powerful when we use it in the circle."

Stillday went through slides that described the following on the Medicine Wheel; the four basic elements, the four directions, the four seasons, the four sacred colors, the four sacred medicines, the four aspects of our being, spiritual, emotional, physical and mental, and the direction of healing, individual, family, community, and nation.

He also placed on the Medicine Wheel the Seven Grandfather Teachings, and the Circle of Life.

"We all walk the Circle of Life from babe to elder, but don't get stuck, my wife sometimes says that I'm stuck in my 'terrible twos,'" said a smiling Stillday.

Stages of life:

- Trust (as a newborn)

- Autonomy (I can do it)

- Initiative (Imagination)

- Accomplishment (I am good)

- Identity (who am? why am I here?)

- Intimacy (able to relate to the world)

- Generosity (giving)

- Integrity (understanding, wisdom)

(Language Summit, PP16)

"If you missed going through any of these stages, they don't go away," noted Chi-Ma'iingan, "they are still there until we go through it. And so we walk the wheel. It started when we were told as young children not to color outside the lines. It's okay to color outside the lines."

"Start to listen to the things of nature," said Stillday. "Our language is in nature and consequently is still in us. Listen to what your heart is talking about. I learn by observing. I watch and then I understand me. When you learn this, everything is alive. If nature is alive then our language is alive. We talked with nature and "they" gave us crap for that, and now "they" talk with geckos," he quipped.

"The youth are fulfilling the Prophesy. We are seeing young people with old spirits, they will sing the old songs. The young are going to the elders and offering asemaa (tobacco), this is appropriate, this is good," Stillday concluded.

At about 4:30 p.m., Gichi-Ma'iingan was asked to do the closing. He made the "closing" short and simple thus ensuring attention. "We are doing as our ancestors did." Larry continued, "The people were asked and then all came together and pooled their wisdom. We're not closing…we are just beginning. Thank you for sharing with me."

Language Summit Presentation

Full Video Transcription

Seven Clans Casino, December 17, 2013

Videotaped by John Parsons, Video Transcription by Me

Culture, Language and the Teachings of the Medicine Wheel.

Boozhoo, Boozhoo,

Aho, boozhoo. (He first introduced himself in Ojibwemowin.) What am I speaking? What am I speaking? Howa! Lotta young kids over there. Good. Ya know, they asked me to speak about our language. You know we call it language. They asked me to speak about Anishinaabe. Now I'm going to do a PowerPoint, and I'd like to have you to participate, by reading that. Now before we go on, you know I just found out why our grandfathers our ancestors a long time ago, why they didn't teach us. Because somebody kept going to them and saying they're not spelling it right.

I'm going to be talking about our language. Can somebody read that for me? Do you know what this is for, to help each other? What does that say?

You know our language; it really didn't go nowhere. The way, I listened to the old people a long time ago, and they would go out, they'd go out in the field, out in the woods. And they'd be out there and sometimes and they'd be talking, like they're talking to themselves. (At least that's what I used to think) Until I found out we have relatives all over, and that's who they were talking to. When they walked out there in the field.

I'm gonna talk about some teachings, some time-honored teachings. These sacred teachings, ya know they didn't go away. They never went away. They didn't go anywhere. So follow along on this PowerPoint. I'm trying to make it so you can visually see as we go through these.

When I first got home, I started putting our language and the teachings on a PowerPoint, and I was told I wasn't supposed to do that. But like I've always done in my life, I didn't listen. I went right ahead and did it. So those of you, my elders here, I apologize. I ask for them for permission to talk about the teachings. That I, myself, learned. And so we're gonna go through this again, I'd like to have you participate.

Who's gonna read that? (Ojibwe slide) Thank you for coming to listen to this. These are the things that we need to begin to do. Make them available to our young kids, for our children, and for ourselves. (Speaks Ojibwe) This is the language we were given. And we were given that language so we could speak to the Creator. We can speak to creation. That's why they give us this language. Susan, (Susan Johnson) can you read that? (Ojibwe) This is the way our language was placed, and it goes back to the Creation Story, and those are the kind of teachings the old people had. The Creation story. 'Cause that's the way they put our language, when they gave us our language.

Number 1, (Ojibwe) when the Creator created life, when He made life, He put everything in a circle. And that includes our language. Our language flows in a circle. How many here teach the language in a linear way? They make you think, they make you memorize that. You know there's something that's really interesting. Very powerful as a matter of fact, our language is very powerful. It is powerful when you put it in a circle. When we use it as a circle. Not because we choose to do it, but because that's the way Gichi-Manidoo put our language.

And everything else in life follows a circular and cyclic pattern. You can tell, when you disconnect yourself from the earth. When you disconnect yourself from the earth, you're going to experience stress, tension, anxiety, headache, and all these things. But we are very fortunate here in Red Lake; our Red Lake people don't have that stuff. They're good people. (Ojibwe)

He kinda gave us everything that we need to make our earth walk. He put it inside us number one, and then he put it out there in nature, in creation.

Somebody gonna read that. (Ojibwe) I can't see that. What does that say? (Ojibwe) Redby, how do you say Redby? Red Lake, Little Rock, and Ponemah…Obaashiing. These districts are laid out in a circle. So when we get to put them in that way, we then start inviting the language. We start inviting the language. My technician over there…(looking at wife Violet) Gichi-Manidoo put lessons everywhere in nature. And this is where our language, Nanabozho was given the task to go name everything in creation, so, he went to Wal-Mart and got a Webster's dictionary and went and named everything in English. No! He put our language in nature, that is where our language is, and when in nature, we…we are nature.

Okay, I'm gonna start looking at the principles. You know keep in mind this is the order of creation. One of the first things He put together were the basic elements, the four basic elements. (Chatter) So what is there? What is there? Noodin, it's the wind. (Ojibwe) These four basic elements are the four elements that all of life consists of. We consist of that, and we depend on those, they can go on forever. We depend on them.

Okay, the four directions. We go to the four directions. (Chatter) That's the direction the winds are blowing from. Okay the four seasons, Spring, Aho! Summer/Niibin. Winter/Biboon. Everything that grows changes like the seasons…even us as individuals. We were given a place on the wheel on our birth month. And this is a good month, we have our own seasons not necessarily in line with the natural seasons, we go through our own seasons. I'll talk about that later.

The Four Colors. (Ojibwe) This is the color of the four races of human beings. Red yellow, black and white, and that the Creator gave the colors when he created the human being. (Chatter) These are the sacred herbs. We use these ceremonial herbs, plants as well as medicinal. So these are just pretty basic, kinda just the surface of our culture, maybe that's a good idea again to name that. You see that Nanabozho named these herbs, and he gave them an Ojibwe name, even the four directions, he gave them Ojibwe names, even the four elements he gave them Ojibwe words. So what does that tell us? Our language is there and it's still alive.

Okay gonna talk about Anishinaabe. Youth, what is a youth? All right. What's this, adult? That excludes me. Okay, up there elder, you see that, and this is the path that all of us have been invited by the Creator to walk. This is the journey that we take on the physical plain, and that's the direction of our growth. And each and every person at the time we're born gets on this path.

Remember I said that last slide there when He made Anishinaabe, he gave them something, he gave them some principles; some laws that they could live with. Gave them seven of them. Can you say that? Aho. Goes through the seven laws. Bravery or courage… Honesty, I can't see that, anybody? See there right at the beginning we were given these laws we were given these to live by. You know when we talk about Mino-bimaadiziwin, (A Good Life) this is what we're talking about, we're talking about these seven laws. We are to live according to these laws and principles. Do the best we can. And one of the things that's really interesting is they didn't go away. These principles did not go away, they are still here.

Now here's one of the things that we stopped doing. (Ojibwe) They had ceremonies for this and these ceremonies were to celebrate the transition of a child as he begins to develop into a young adult, childhood young adult all the way up. Now these ceremonies (Ojibwe) that's what our people know, they knew that. And they started from the beginning with Trust of an infant. An infant comes into this world already has that Trust. And one of the first things an infant will do is to begin to look around and say is this world safe? If that world is safe for that infant then that infant will say I wanna be here, I like it here.

And then he goes down to the next one, Autonomy. And we gave a name for that you know what that is? The Terrible Twos! A lot of people are there huh? I am. I'm still in my terrible twos. I'm running all over and trying to get people to acknowledge me. To tell me I'm somebody. Do we have people like that? Now that has got to be completed. At that time, the terrible twos, a little two-year old right, is trying to claim his independence. Hey I am somebody, I am about somebody, and here then comes grandma/auntie, little two year old stands there watching and this big person comin' up, scoop 'em up, and the little person going…where's my independence, was that a violation? It could be.

Then we move down to the third one. Initiative. See these are what…our grandpas and grandmas, they knew this. They knew as they watched a child begin to develop, and they were there at each transition with a ceremony. And that child continued to develop and begin to feel good. That child needed to have that sense of feeling good.

Because it needed it…they were needed for the fourth one, Accomplishment. Accomplishment doesn't mean doing something and accomplishing something, this kind of accomplishment is being good at being. I am somebody. I am good. That's what that accomplishment means. And that child, that child needs to have that because the next phase will be Identity.

That's where that child will begin to answer three questions. Who am I? Why am I here? Where am I going? That child has to answer those. If he don't, he's gonna get stuck there. And we have a lot of our people stuck, they go to one another and say tell me something, tell me I'm good. Give me an Identity. So when they had the ceremonies for those, the child knew who he or she was.

Then they move up to the next phase. That's Intimacy. Now this type of intimacy is to be able to relate to the world as adult to adult. If you do not complete any of the previous ones, you're gonna get stuck there. You will always be treating like adult to child. That's how you'll be functioning, you'll be relating to life. And if you succeed, you'll get up to the seventh one, Generosity.

That Generosity is to be able to give and take. Somebody comes to give you something, you say thank you. Don't do like I do, somebody comes to give something and I say "Ahhh you shouldn't have done that, now I owe you something." That kind of generosity is to say thank you. It's give and take. Then the last one is Integrity.

Talk to them old people, they told me what they talk about, "Tell me about this," they said, that's when the snow is on top of the mountain. By that time you should have at least some understanding about life and yourself. And you have some knowledge and wisdom.

See these are the ceremonies our people had. How many remember them? They used to have them. Susan, do you remember them? (Ojibwe) The ceremony? See that's what we need to get back. We need to get our children back on that line. Because if you miss these; they won't go away.

Don't be like me, 73 years old. (He was 69) And I'm still fighting for identity. Identity is calling me. It's inside here. They are saying we've got to be completed. That is why our people they had ceremonies for those things. And when they had the ceremonies it helped the child go into the next phase, a transition. On these ceremonies (Ojibwe) they also had a space there to breathe. Because when you leave the former state, you're naturally gonna try to get back to the natural state. But the elders they helped them grieve that, then let it go. You're in a new place; you're a new person.

These have to be successfully completed. And if our children miss something, you know we can give them this. We can start doing that for them. And I guarantee you that will help them.

Okay, this is the Four Aspects of Our Being. This is who we are. What does that say? (Ojibwe) Physical, that's the body. That's the physical body. Okay what's that say? Okay, she knows them. She's doing a good job over there. (Probably Susan Ninham) I think this is something that we need to give to our kids. They can see that - and that is one of our teachings.

Our earliest teachings they had the baby, they used to put them on that…I call it torture rack. What did they call that little baby thing? Oh, adikinaagan. How many guys remember that? I do, I still got mine. I lay in it every night. They put that baby in there. Number one they wrap them up. Why did they wrap them up? Time… So they won't pick their nose. No, it gives them that feeling of that womb, in the mother's womb. When they were in the womb for nine months and then one day the doctor pulls them out. Do you ever see them? They're just reaching, they're reaching and kicking; they're looking for that wall. That safety. So when they wrapped them up like that it reminds them. Remember that first principle up there is trust, to be safe.

But that little adikinaagan you know that's really neat that somebody really was a genius to come up with that. They got that thing that's over the head with that dip on it, I used to wonder what that was. Then I found out. The baby's on the mother's back when she's out there doing her daily chores, they put the baby against the tree. For what? (Ojibwe) Look at your relatives; you got relatives everywhere.

You guys, you ever see a baby go out they just love to get in that sand. Do you know what they're doing? They're having a relationship with Earth Mother. They still have that close relationship. So they get out there and they just roll in that sand. And today mother runs into the house with a washrag, huh phoo. Is that the beginning of the disconnection?

When we're looking at being disconnected, then you get up, get up into school; you give a child a box of crayons. I remember the first box that I got. There were 64 of them in there. And I was like a millionaire, because with those 64 crayons I could create magic. Ever see the kids with a crayon? They just paint magic. Then suddenly grandma who was an A student all her school, "Between the lines, you gotta stay between the lines." The little baby looks up and says, "Okay grandma, I'll stay in a box for the rest of my life."

You know these are the kind of things that changed throughout time. A lotta things about our lives changed, but these didn't. These principles did not change. And again, I said this is just the surface, the surface information.

When I first started, when I first started to understand the four directions, I say, "Hey Waabanong (East), hey Zhaawanong (South), hey Ningaabii'an (West), hey Giiwedin (North)." Man I was a holy man. I was a very traditional person because I knew the four directions. And then the old people started talking to me, bizindan (Listen to it). That was one of the first things, bizindan. And I really didn't know what they were talking about. But they just kept saying, bizindan; bizindan. Finally, I understood what that meant. I started to listen. I started to listen to things out there in nature. And it seems like the things I was hearing out there, were happening simultaneously inside. And that is where our language is. It's still in us. It's in all of us.

Forget about how to say plastic in Ojibwe. Because what does that mean anyway? Quit trying to say kangaroo. This is what your heart is talking about, because it talks to us all the time. We need to get to that place where we can be quiet. And that could be anywhere. It's different for each of us. Some like it by the water, or by the rocks, some go out into the woods. How many here go to Walmart? Get a spiritual awakening at Walmart. Ha, good sale!

This is what we were given. You know I showed this here, these slides ya know, because it's out there. It's out there; you can see these things out there. And you can go be with these things out there. And one of the other things, maybe this is just the way I learned, I learned by observing. I watch, that's the way that I began to learn. I began to understand that way. Not that I understand everything in life, there's only one thing that I have come to understand. Just one. And that's me. Once you understand yourself, these things will come alive. They are alive. All that stuff out in nature is alive. And since nature is alive, that means our language is alive.

Visit my grandmother, on my Dad's side. She used to take us out into the woods; ya know, go out there and pick raspberries. Of course you know as a kid, I didn't pay much attention. But then one day I began to realize I'm going to listen to her. And she'd go out there and she knew exactly where these raspberries would be abundant. She was talking to those raspberries. She was talking to them, to them plants. See that's what our people do, we talk with nature. And they punish us for that. And now today those people talk to geckos. They talk to geckos and they even put it on TV. And they said we shouldn't be talking to plants, but that is who we are as people.

And before I quit I'm going to acknowledge Sam and the crew. These are the guys that are working. How about the committees ya got Sam? If you are on the committee stand up. These are the people; these are the ones who are leading the way. These are the ones who are putting together the foundation, and I talked to them at one time at a meeting. And they didn't realize it then, that they were fulfilling a prophecy. One of the old prophecies said young people will be born with old spirits. Young people will be going to the drum and singing the old songs. Young people will go to the elders and start asking, asking for directions. And this is what these young people are doing. I'm very proud of them. Aho miigwech.

If you want copies of these slides they're on sale at Walmart.

Path of Life, PP03

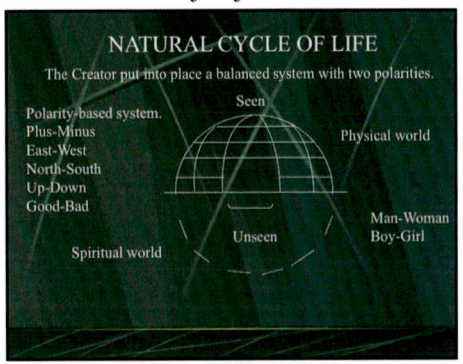

Cycle of Life, PP02

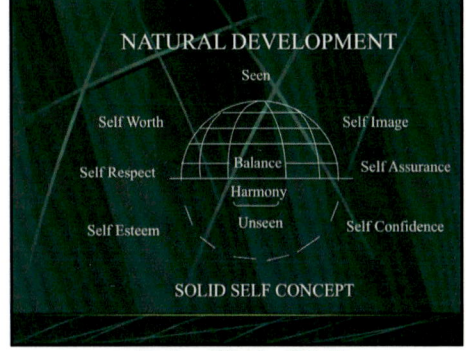

Cycle of Life, PP07

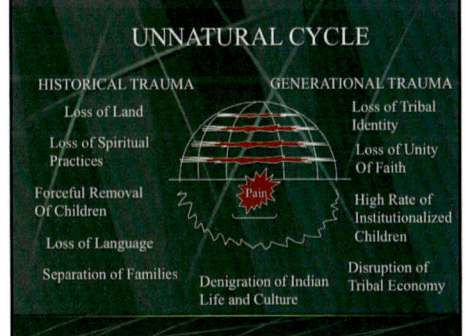

Cycle of Life, PP09

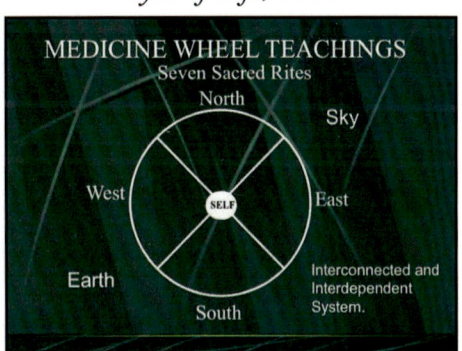

Med Wheel 7 Teach PP08

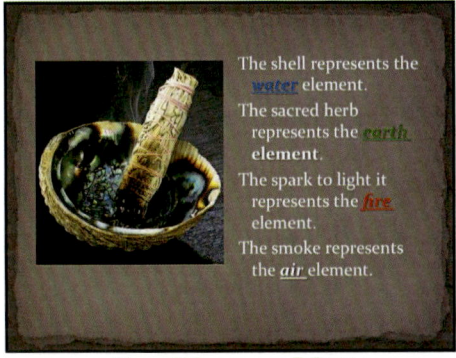

Four Elements, PP03

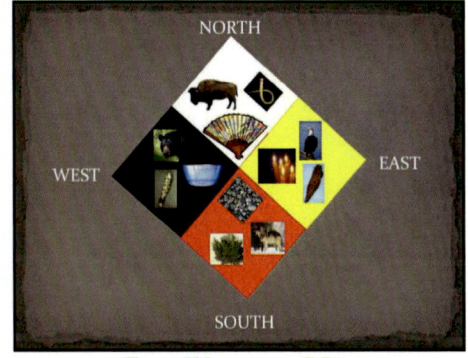

Four Elements, PP23

PowerPoint Inserts

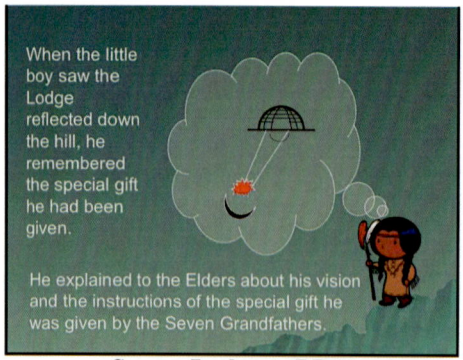

Sweat Lodge 1, PP43

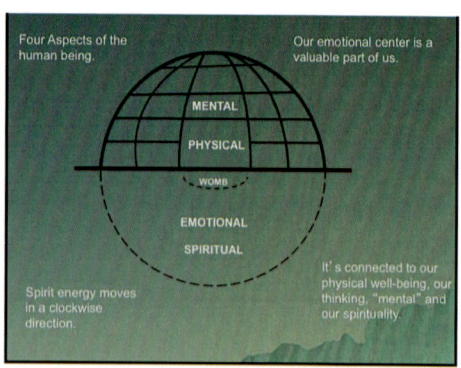

Sweat Lodge 1, PP48

Sweat Lodge 2, PP02

Sweat Lodge 2, PP05

Sweat Lodge 2, PP06

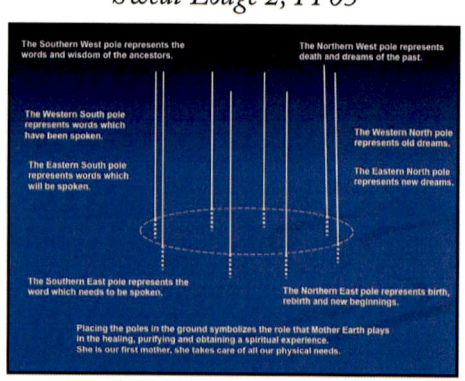

Sweat Lodge 2, PP22

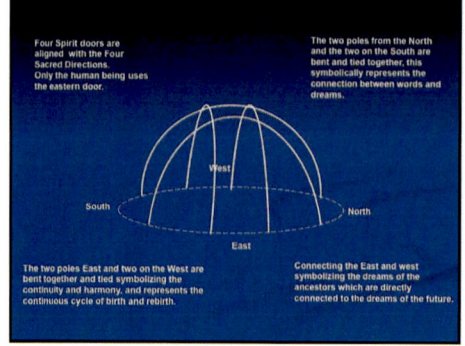

Sweat Lodge 2, PP23

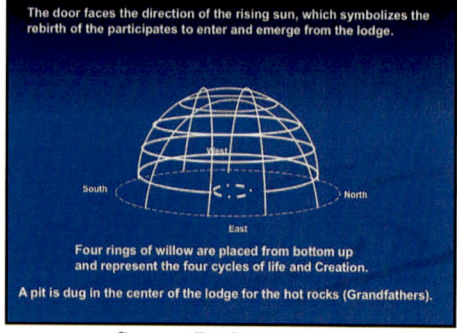

Sweat Lodge2, PP24

PowerPoint Inserts

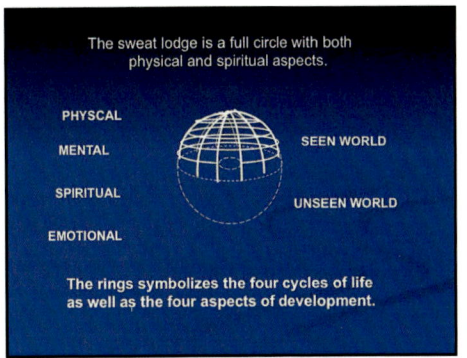

Sweat Lodge 2, PP25

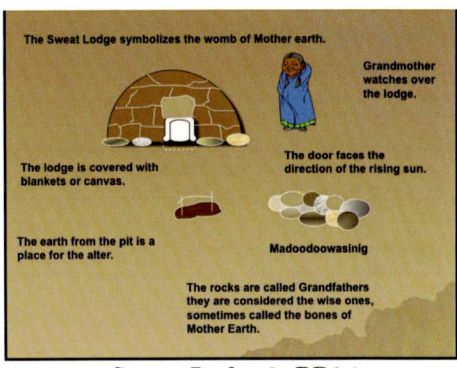

Sweat Lodge 2, PP26

Sweat Lodge 2, PP28

Sweat Lodge 3, PP01

Sweat Lodge 3, PP05

Sweat Lodge 3, PP06

Sweat Lodge 3, PP07

Sweat Lodge 3, PP08

PowerPoint Inserts

Sweat Lodge 3, PP26

Sweat Lodge 3, PP29

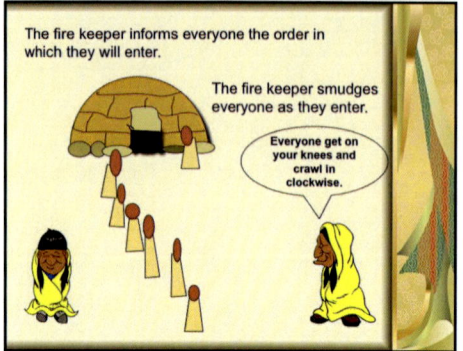

Sweat Lodge 3, PP35

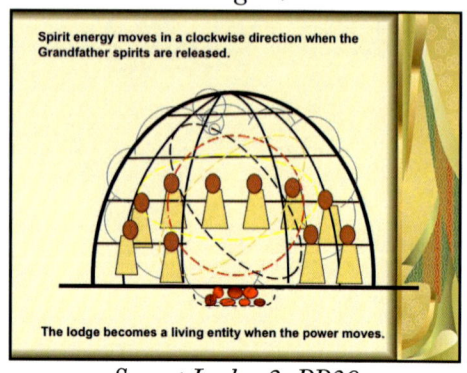

Sweat Lodge 3, PP39

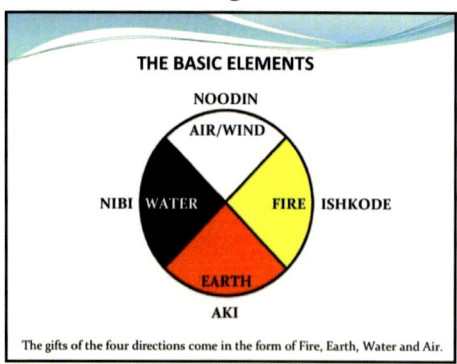

Multi Teachings 1, PP20

Multi Teachings 1, PP31

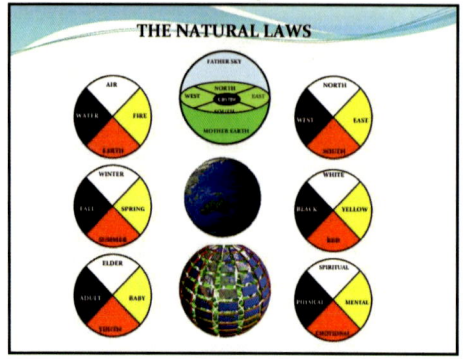

Multi Teachings 1, PP46

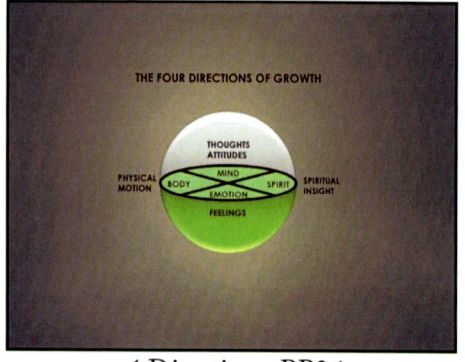

4 Directions, PP24

PowerPoint Inserts

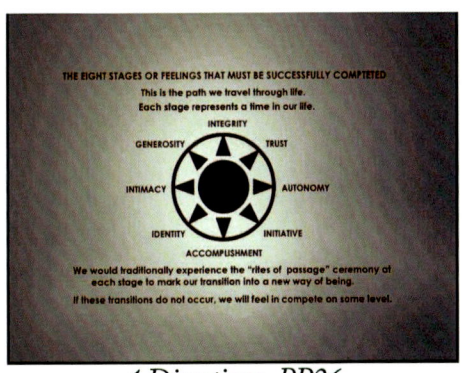

4 Directions, PP26

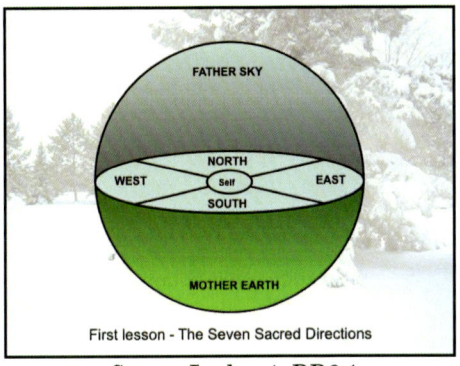

Language Summit PP16

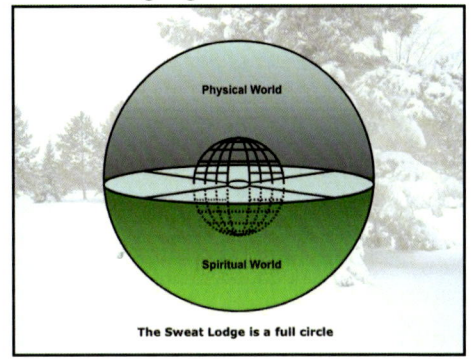

Sweat Lodge 4, PP04

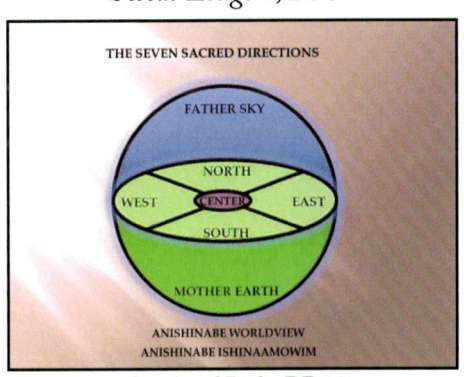

Sweat Lodge 4, PP05

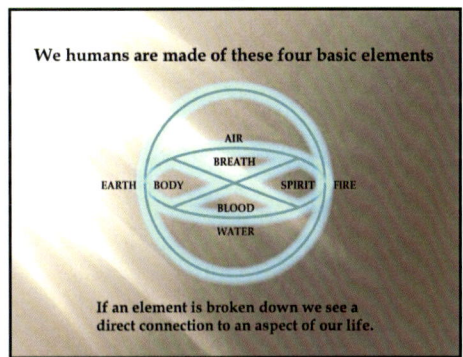

Circle of Life, PP19

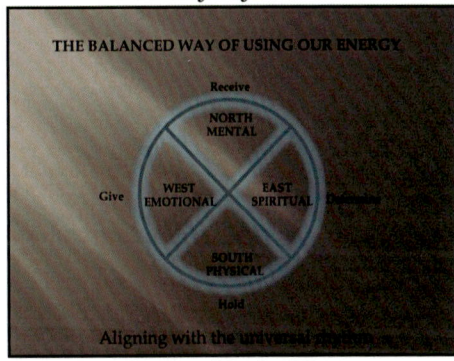

Circle of Life, PP25

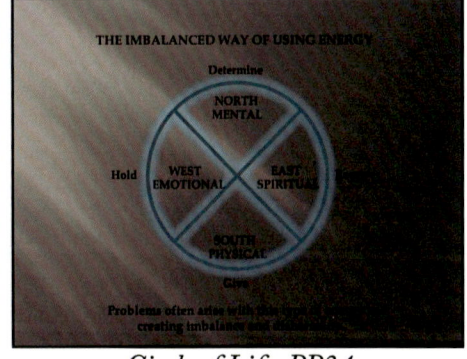

Circle of Life, PP33

Circle of Life, PP34

PowerPoint Inserts

Ancient Wisdom for Modern Times (3)

February 2014

Story Written March 2, 2014

Ancient Wisdom for Modern Times: The Seven Teachings

Presentation at 8th Annual Drug & Gang Summit

"Gigitiziiwaan, Ochibajiganan ingii, Miinigozimin" (Family – A Sacred Gift)

Ancient Wisdom for Modern Times

Gwayako-bimaadiziwin (The Right Kind of Life)

"We are invited once again to revisit the time honored Teachings, and to embrace the old ways in order to renew our connection to the Sacred Teachings. We need this old knowledge in our lives to live in these modern times of technology."

So began a PowerPoint presentation by Gichi-Ma'iingan/Big Wolf (Larry Stillday) - aided by wife Violet - at the 8th Annual Drug and Gang Summit held at Seven Clans Casino and Event Center on February 11 to 13, 2014. Stillday would make this presentation on both Tuesday and Wednesday.

"Gigi-mini-goomiin gakina gegoo gi-mino-bimdiziyang mewizha," (A long time ago, we were given everything we need to live a good life) he said. "We are taught that we originated from the Earth and that the Earth is the Great Mother of all, She provides us with everything we need to survive in this life."

The Cycle of Life

"Everything was put in place for our earth walk," said Stillday. "Our earth walk begins when our spirit enters our physical body from the direction of the East. The traditional way of teaching was by example, experience and story-telling. Learning is a continuous process from birth to death."

Stillday says that there are many lessons we can learn from the natural world, because that's where the Great Spirit put all the lessons we need to fulfill our earth walk. We were given everything to live a good life.

"When we put our frame of reference of thinking on our Earth Mother, and look deep into nature, we have a better understanding of everything," he said. "When we connect with the animal guides, they help us to be a better person, and to be healthier spiritually, emotionally, physically and mentally. This enables us to see the world and everything in it with clarity and better understanding. We need to plug into the earth!"

"The Circle is one of the strongest symbols in nature," declared Gichi-Ma'iingan. "Symbolism is the most powerful language that we were given to understand and communicate with spiritual concepts and truths. Our Ancestors always engaged in ceremonies as a way of honoring all of life; they thrived on symbolism to help them see the world in terms of circles and cycles. Like them, we too can use the same framework of symbolism to incorporate the circular and spiral energies."

"The Medicine Wheel is the symbol we use to express and represent the meaning of life, and meaning provides us with purpose and understanding. The symbol of the circle holds a special place of importance in our belief system. There is no hierarchy in a circle, it's about equality."

Ceremonies Are Our First Duty

"The greatest wisdom is in simplicity," he said. "It is not complex or elaborate and is encoded in our DNA. Everything we need is within; therefore we are programed for ceremonies and rituals, which is our inheritance from our Ancestors.

"When we quit doing our ceremony something else comes in, fills the gap. But when we engage in our ceremonies, we awaken and affirm our innate wisdom and we invoke our ability to heal mind, body, heart and spirit. We are born into the natural rhythm of the Universe and Mother Earth, which connects us with our own natural rhythm, and with Nature. The great teachers have always said, 'When we find our heart, we will find our way.'"

"For us to live Mino-Bimaadiziwin (the Good Life), we need to return to the Teachings and our way of understanding. The Mino-Bimaadiziwin Principles provide the outline of what it means to live and learn as Anishinaabeg," said Stillday.

The Seven Natural Laws for a Good Life, or the Seven Principles
Niizhwaaso-nimishoomis-gikinoo'amaagewiinon
(The Seven Grandfather Teachings)

Stillday says that the Aadizookaanaan (Sacred Stories) tell us the Great Spirit gave the Seven Grandfathers, who are very powerful spirits, the responsibility to watch over the people.

"The Teachings of the Seven Grandfathers were given to us early in our history. They are teachings about human conduct towards others," said Stillday. "The teachings are important and have long been a part of our language. They have been handed down to us through generations. They are gifts or blueprints for living a good life. Each teaching is a gift of knowledge for the learning of values and living by those values. They were given to us in order to develop the spiritual aspect of self, and to teach us the importance for understanding who we are. The teachings were then, and still are, what we need for our families and our communities to survive and thrive."

Stillday says the concepts of Respect and Sharing that forms the foundation of a way of life, are based on the Seven Grandfather Teachings. Each teaching provides the framework for a good way of life.

"All of our feelings, thoughts and actions are a combination of one or more or even all of the Seven Teachings," said Stillday. "The Teachings remind us of the need for balance in the world, and the balance we must strive for everyday within ourselves. The teachings offer direction for all who wish to have a balanced and peaceful life."

"Our wisdom keepers say, we are to use all these laws together in our lives and NOT to pick and choose between them," said Stillday, "because to pick and choose one, will only work the opposite way of what is intended. When we break one law, we break all of them because they all work together in balance. When we break one law of the Great Spirit we not only break the law with the Great Spirit, we break the law with ourselves, our families and our communities."

"Each law honors the basic virtue necessary for a full and healthy life. The teachings honor spiritual laws that help us connect to the land," he said.

An Animal represents each Teaching

"The Seven Grandfather Teachings are intended to work in a Circle, equally together," said Stillday. "The Circle has always been an important part of our everyday lives. Everyone and everything in the circle is equal, as well as interconnected, which helps us to have a strong sense of family and community."

"The teachings emphasize the importance of respect for all," says Stillday. "Animals are here to help man. The animals taught us how to live close to the earth, and that connection we have with them, instilled the respect for all of life. Each animal offers a special gift and understanding of how we are to live our lives on Mother Earth."

Nibwaakaawin (Wisdom) is represented by Amik (Beaver)

Amik represents determination, strong will, gathering and accomplishment. To cherish knowledge is to know Wisdom. We were given Wisdom in order to better our lives through knowledge. To know Wisdom is to know that the Great Spirit gave everyone special gifts to be used to build a strong family and a healthy community. Developing a strong family and a community is entirely dependent on the gifts given to each individual by the Great Spirit, and how we use those gifts.

Amik uses its sharp teeth to cut trees and branches to build its dams and lodges, a gift it received from the Great Spirit. Amik teaches us the lesson of Wisdom in the way it uses its teeth or gift to build its lodges for its family; if it doesn't use its teeth, they will continue to grow and become useless, making it difficult to sustain its life. It is the same way for us. If we let our own spirit go weak, it will not be able to fulfill its use. Like the beaver if we use our gifts properly, they will greatly contribute to the development of a healthy family and community.

Zaagi'idiwin (Love) is represented by Migizi (Bald Eagle)

Migizi was chosen by the Great Spirit to represent this teaching. To know true Love is to know the Great Spirit. To have Love is to know peace. The Love we give the Great Spirit is expressed through the love of one's self. It has been said that if one cannot love one's self, it is impossible to love anyone else.

Love is something we must have because our spirit feeds on it; without it we become weak, our self-esteem becomes weak. Without Love our courage fails, and without Love we will not be able to look at the world with confidence. But with Love, we are creative, and live with endless energy, and with it, and it alone, we are more able to sacrifice for others.

Minwaadendamowin (Respect) is represented by Mashkode Bizhiki (Buffalo/Bison)

To honor all of Creation is to have Respect. The attributes of the Mashkode Bizhiki are: Sacredness, abundance, stamina, sacrifice and provider. The giving of its life showed the deep Respect it had for the people. Its gift provided shelter, clothing, and utensils for daily living. It established a sustainable relationship resulting in an expression of True Respect.

The essence of respect is to give. To show respect to life is to give of yourself. You must give respect if you wish to be respected. Accepting everyone without judgment is the way respecting the Great Spirit works.

Aakwade'ewin (Bravery or Courage) is represented by Makwa (Bear)

Bravery is facing the most difficult situation with integrity. Makwa offers many teachings in the way it lives. Bravery is the most important teaching it offers, although gentle by nature, it will become ferocious if her cubs are approached which teaches a true definition of Bravery. Makwa teaches us the lesson that in order to have the mental and moral strength to overcome our fears that prevent us from living our true spirit, is the greatest challenge we must meet with the same intensity as the mother bear protecting her cubs. Living of the heart and spirit is difficult, but the Bear's example shows us how to face danger to achieve our goals.

Makwa represents Courage through its strength and natural ability to overcome the challenges it faces. A mother bear will stand up against a much stronger male bear or other threats to protect her cubs. Just as the bear hibernates during the winter and awakes in the spring, we too need rest and rejuvenation. Makwa teaches us the lesson about how to live a balanced life, and a time to be playful and a time to be assertive and courageous. Makwa calls us to awaken our full potential and to stand up for what we believe.

Gwekowaadiziwin (Honesty) is represented by Misaabe (Sasquatch or Big Foot)

Misaabe represents the essence of Honesty. Misaabe reminds us about the importance of being Honest with each other and Honesty in facing difficult situations bravely. To be truly Honest, is to keep the promises made to the Great Spirit, to others, and to one's self.

Honesty means being an honorable person free of fraud and deception. The Elders say: "The highest honor that can be given to a person is someone saying, 'There goes an honest person who can be trusted.' The wisdom keepers say, 'Never try to be someone else, live true to your spirit, be Honest to yourself, and accept yourself the way you are, the way the Great Spirit made you.'"

Dibaadendiziwin (Humility) is represented by Ma'iingan (Wolf)

Humility is to know yourself as a Sacred part of Creation. Ma'iingan represents loyalty, perseverance and intuition. Recognizing and acknowledging there is a power greater than ourselves is to be truly Humble. The expression of Humility is shown through the consideration of others before ourselves. We are to never consider ourselves to be superior or inferior to anyone.

In nature, Ma'iingan is the teacher of Humility. Ma'iingan will bow its head, not out of fear but out of Humbleness, in our presence. When Ma'iingan hunts for food, it will take it back to the den for the others before it eats. Each Ma'iingan has a place in the whole and yet maintains its individual personality.

Debwewin (Truth) is represented by Mikinaak (Turtle)

To know Truth is to know and understand all seven of the original Grandfather Teachings and remain faithful to all of them. The shell of Mikinaak represents the body of real events as created by the Great Spirit, and serves as a reminder of the Creator's will and teachings.

There are 13 markings on the back of Mikinaak which represent the 13 moons, which represents the Truth of one cycle of the earth's rotation around the sun, and the four seasons. There are also 28 markings that represent the cycle of one moon. Mikinaak was present at the time the Seven Grandfather Teachings were given. It is Turtle's responsibility to ensure that they will never be lost or forgotten.

How Do We Live Right?

The teachings are not ancient, they never went away, so we ask, who moved? We need these Teachings now more than ever. Following the Teachings leads to well-being and onto a good path in life. The Wisdom Keepers say, to heal the Nation we must first heal the individual, family then community. And it's for anybody and everybody.

The teachings are meant to work together, that's why they are in a Circle. If they were linear, they become a memory. When we break one heart, we break them all, as they are interconnected. If you don't have balance, you are part of the problem, because it's an interconnected system. The Teachings help us find that balance.

The Spirits come out at certain times of the year, they look to the left and to the right. They are looking for ceremony. They come back to see if we are awake. We need the medicine of 'living right.' Manidoog (the Spirits) are looking for the ceremony by the Lake. When they see that, that's when the teaching comes.

A Healing Ceremony was held at the end of the Drug & Gang Summit.

Taking Care of Mother Earth (4)

Presented April 10, 2014 34 slides

Story Written June 1, 2014

The Last Public Teaching of Gichi-Ma'iingan

Ten Days after the death of Larry Stillday, still grieving, I wrote the story of his last teaching entitled "Taking Care of Mother Earth." It was well received and made a headline in the National publication *Indian Country Today*, where it had over 2,000 shares on social media.

The Teaching was held on April 10, 2014 at what was billed as a Culture/Language Revitalization Event Held at Red Lake Middle School. Larry turned 70 years old on May 14, and died on May 20, 2014.

Preface to "Taking Care of Mother Earth"

What follows is the last "public" teaching of Gichi-Ma'iingan. While Larry Stillday left us on May 20, 2104, Gichi-Ma'iingan - "Gaa-izhinikaanid"(the one who named me) - lives on in the hearts and minds of not only the Red Lake people, but in the minds of all four colors of the Medicine Wheel who heard or read his words.

He often said of his teachings, "It's not about Indians, it's about people! The other colors will come to us and we must share. All the life forces must come into alignment! The Prophecies tell us that we are now in the time of great healing. It says the four Colors of the human family are once again given an opportunity to bring each Color's gifts together and create a mighty nation."

Many walked with Larry and benefited by his teachings. We all remember his messages. One that comes to mind at this time seems to resonate. At the end of what was to become the first of five Healing Lodges held at "Obaashiing University" Larry said, "Gigaagiigidotamaagoom, maada'ooyok gaa-miinigooyeg." (You are speakers for us now. Share what you have learned)

With a heavy heart, I submit.

Biidaanakwad (Gathering Cloud) Michael Meuers, Bemijigamaag

Culture/Language Event Held at Red Lake School
"Taking Care of Mother Earth" is Theme
Story and Photos by Michael Meuers

"Taking care of Mother Earth comes from the fact we were given the responsibility as caretaker of the earth. Since we are of the earth — to take care of Mother Earth - we do that by taking care of ourselves. It's an interconnected, interdependent and interrelated system. Since we have become separated from the earth, we are separated within ourselves too." ~Gichi-Ma'iingan

The Teaching was held appropriately in the Culture Room of the Red Lake Middle School. The teacher, Midewinini Gichi-Ma'iingan would speak of symbols in a room full of symbols. It was Thursday, April 10, 2014. The air outside was cool, due to a tardy spring, on the Red Lake Indian Reservation.

But a certain warmth and calmness claims all those who enter the circular, colorful, and rustic room. A variety of seating is available…log and half-log furniture, tables, benches and chairs. Pipes, hand drums, paintings, birch bark, and other Ojibwe crafts dot the circular wall. Minnesota and MIA banners border eagle staffs, along with US and Red Lake Nation flags. They all stand to the left of Migizi.

High on the walls seated on platforms are sculptures depicting Red Lake's seven major clans. Below each symbol was the name of the clan written in Ojibwemowin; Makwa (Bear) Mikinaak (Turtle), Awaazisii (Bullhead), Waabizheshi (Marten), Migizi (Bald Eagle), Ojiig (Fisher), and Ogiish-kimanisii (Kingfisher).

As people trickle into the room after enjoying a light supper in the high school cafeteria, they are greeted by a cheerful middle school principle before taking a seat facing a screen.

The image on the screen is familiar to some as a photo taken in the woods near Obaashiing, the site of Obaashiing University and the many Wellness Camps hosted by Larry and Violet Stillday. A sweat lodge and large Medicine Wheel are prominent. (The next Wellness Camp had been slated for June 10, 2014) The wife of the evening's tutor, Violet Stillday, operates the PowerPoint presentation, entitled "Taking Care of Mother Earth".

To the right of the screen stood her husband, spiritual advisor and teacher, Gichi-Ma'iingan (Larry Stillday), who commented on how appropriate it was to have this teaching in a circular room surrounded by clan symbols.

"My how we have become detached from ourselves! We are spirits having a human experience, not humans trying to be spiritual. We are here to complete that human experience," ~Gichi-Ma'iingan.

"Our culture and are language are still here because our land is still here. This is where the Creator put it, on the land. Our ancestors are waiting for us." ~Gichi-Ma'iingan.

"Taking Care of Mother Earth"

Wellness

"Many of us have been brought up to believe that our health depends solely on the quality of healthcare we receive," began Gichi-Ma'iingan. "The truth is we are responsible for our health. We are the ones who make lifestyle decisions that contribute to our well-being."

Stillday emphasized that we, as individuals, are the ones that must take the steps to take care of our health and promote our wellness. "The power is within us to create the wellness in our lives," he said.

Disconnected

"We have been taught, and continue to be influenced to think, in terms of pieces of ideas and concepts rather than in integrated terms of ideas and concepts, which is more in line with our way of learning," Stillday carefully explained.

"Thinking this way has led us to look at our spiritual, emotional, physical and mental aspects of our being as if each aspect is completely separated, rather than being interconnected with each other," he said.

Stillday explained that thinking this way has led us to look at our health in a compartmentalized way, rather than in a management way of the whole being.

State of Imbalance

"Thinking in this way has led us to think as if our bodies, organs and systems are separated from our thoughts, emotions and spirit." This is a state of imbalance.

State of Balance

"For us, health is more than the absence of disease, it is a state of optimal well-being." This is a state of balance. "The way we were given to think and learn, gives us that power within ourselves to create the wellness we need in our lives. That power is the power of choice."

Optimal Well-being

"For us, (tribal peoples) optimal well-being is a concept of health that goes beyond the curing of illness to one of achieving Mino-Aayaawin or Wellness," said Gichi-Ma'iingan. "We are given everything we need, these instructions have not changed."

"Achieving wellness requires balancing the four aspects of our whole being, this holistic approach involves integrating all four aspects as an ongoing process."

Stillday's PowerPoint then flashed several statements on the screen, first in Ojibwemowin then translated to English.

Mino-aayaawin gigiminigoomin gakina gegoom ji-gwayako bimodiziyaang!

"We were given everything to live right!"

Gayganawendamoog gigiminigoomin miinawaa gayizhiga-nawenidizoyaag!

"We were given what to take care of, and how to take care of ourselves!"

And, as is often the case with Gichi-Ma'iingan, he adds some whimsy.

Boozhoo Endinawemaganidoog awegonnen ishpiming?

"Whad up?" He then added, "How to say camel or kangaroo, what difference does that make?"

Gigi oshisidamagoomin gakayaa gayishiganawendadizooyaan!

"Everything was put in place about how we are to take care of ourselves!"

Giwinjigadawan o'wnowen gayganawendamoog…

"The four aspects of our being (starting in the east then clockwise; spirit, emotion, body, and mind) that we are to take care of were given a name. Nita-awigi'iwewin maajiigi." (The growth/development of being)

"We use the Circle to explain life, and we use the ancient symbol of the Medicine Wheel to illustrate the Cycle of Life," Stillday went on. "To understand the Cycle of Life, we must first understand the teachings of the Medicine Wheel." He then added, "Some think this is a religion, but it's a symbol, a teaching tool."

"We Use the Medicine Wheel Symbol to Represent A Non-Linear Model of Human Development."

"Each direction on the wheel offers lessons and gifts that support the human developmental stages," Stillday explained. "The lesson is to remain balanced at the center of the wheel while developing equally the spiritual, emotional, physical and mental aspects of one's being. To make circles you have to be in the center."

"Our Life Consists of Four Aspects of Existence," said Stillday. "We have to seek balance, wholeness and fulfillment in our lives. We need to heal, develop, and integrate the four aspects within our lives."

Stillday said that using the four interdependent directions of the Medicine Wheel is a holistic approach for living in a good way, and a model for a cultural and traditional lifestyle.

"If anything is Sacred, it is the Human Body. Hold Yourself Sacred!"

"The four aspects of our being also have boundaries," said Gichi-Ma'iingan. "Our (personal) boundaries protect us and give us a sense of who we are; they are not fixed, we change them with what we feel and who we are with."

"When our boundaries are intact we know we have feelings, thoughts and realities that are separate from others! Our boundaries tell us where we end, and where the other person begins."

Stillday noted that developing personal boundaries is one of the core issues for achieving a healthy balanced life. The four aspects (spirit, emotion, body, and mind) and the personal boundaries that each separate aspect contains are what gives us identity and connects us to our innermost self.

Stillday provided some detail.

Spiritual Boundaries: relate to our beliefs, experiences, and our relationship with our Creator.

Emotional Boundaries: distinguishes our emotion and responsibilities in relation to others. It draws an imaginary line or a force field that separates us from others.

Physical Boundaries: our physical space, and privacy.

Mental Boundaries: applies to our values, opinions, attitudes, and thoughts.

Gichi-Ma'iingan went on to say that healthy boundaries give us self-respect, self-esteem, self-image, and self-worth. They give us confidence and a solid self-concept. "This empowers us to make good choices and take responsibility for ourselves, always keeping the *self* at the center of the Wheel.

In The Four States of Being: we bring balance to our lives by honoring our spirit, heart, body and mind. We develop a solid self-concept. (By knowing ours, and respecting others', boundaries)

In The Four Aspects of Health: we are reminded that, 'Well-being' is an ongoing endeavor, not a destination. The four aspects of health (for spirit, heart, body and mind) must be kept in harmony and balance to obtain optimum health, Stillday said.

The Spiritual Aspect

"This is our inner essence," explained Gichi-Ma'iingan, "the part of us that exists beyond time and space and connects us to the Universal Source and to the Oneness of Life."

"Developing our awareness of our spiritual level gives us the experience of a feeling of belonging in the universe and gives us a deeper meaning and purpose."

"Our spiritual aspect provides the foundation for the development of the other three aspects. It develops our relationship with our selves, with our creativity, our life purpose, and our relationship with our Creator."

The Emotional Aspect

"This gives us the ability to experience life on a deeper level," declared Stillday. "It gives us the ability to relate to one another including the world on a deeper level. It's the part of us that seeks meaningful connection and contact with others."

"Developing our emotional aspect (and knowing/applying its boundaries) allows us to feel a wide range of human experience with our five senses and find fulfillment in our relationships with ourselves and others. This aspect is about our feelings, our range of emotions from fear to anger, love to happiness and joy."

"Emotional well-being is not the absence of emotions, but our ability to understand and value our emotions, and to use them to move us forward toward positive directions."

The Physical Aspect

"Our body is a vehicle we have been given so we can experience the world," Stillday noted. "It also includes our ability to survive and thrive in the material world."

"Developing our physical aspect involves learning to take care of our body and enjoying it. It also means developing skills to live comfortably and effectively in the material world," he added.

The Mental Aspect

"This is our intellect," said Stillday, "our ability to think and reason; it also consists of our thoughts, attitudes, beliefs and our values."

"It can be our greatest gift or sometimes our greatest curse. It can cause us to have terrible confusion or bring us profound understanding."

"Developing our mental aspect allows us to think clearly, to be open-minded and to gather knowledge and wisdom through our life experiences from the world around us," he said.

All Four Aspects of our Being are Equally Important

"In order to feel whole and lead a satisfying life we need to spend time and attention on understanding, developing and integrating each aforementioned aspect."

"All of these aspects must work together to make us a whole person. What happens to one aspect affects all the other aspects," Stillday asserted. "Since all four aspects must work in harmony to achieve wellness, each aspect needs our attention and care to perform at its best."

"**The Spiritual you:** requires inner calmness, openness to creativity and trust with your inner knowing."

"**The emotional you:** needs to give and receive forgiveness, love and compassion, needs to laugh and experience happiness."

"**The Physical you:** requires good nutrients, exercise and adequate rest."

"**The Mental you:** needs self-supportive attitudes, positive thoughts and viewpoints, and a positive self-image."

So then…"Health is defined as a Balance Among the Four Aspects of Being," said Stillday. "Reaching a balance in life is an ongoing process."

"Our well-being encompasses all of our parts, not just the physical body; however, taking care of our physical body is an important element in caring for our whole self," Gichi-Ma'iingan said in closing. "It is important to listen to our body because it tells us when it needs our attention; pain is one of those indicators."

Stillday noted that with so much going on in our everyday lives it's easy to get sidetracked; this is why it's important that we remember to try and lead a balanced life.

"One of easiest things we tend forget is how everything within us is connected," Stillday said. "We must continue giving equal time to those four areas of our lives, because if one or more suffers from lack of attention, they will all suffer causing imbalance and disharmony."

Gichi-Ma'iingan, near closing, left us with a teaser on ceremony and how it helps us to achieve balance of the four aspects and boundaries. He thought perhaps he would teach more of its value, perhaps at the next Wellness Camp, sadly never to be.

"There is great value to Aadizookaanaan, (a sacred story), it helps us develop the aspects and is often used in Manidookewin. (Ceremony) Manidookewin is about integrity, the balance of Spirit, Heart, Body, and Mind. It is like a four cylinder engine, ya gotta be hittin' on all cylinders.

"Ceremony is to celebrate the new phases of our lives. It also celebrates when we can't figure the rest. Healing and ceremony push you in the direction you need to heal yourself, not someone else. Sometimes we do things with Manidookewin, but we are the ceremony. How is it they say? 'We are the ones we've been waiting for?'"

"'That's your song. We are talking about rhythm. Happiness comes from the inside, not the outside," said Gichi-Ma'iingan.

Epilogue

Baanimaa (Later, after a while) Gichi-Ma'iingan

"Gigaagiigidotamaagoom, maada'ooyok gaa-miinigooyeg." (You are speakers for us now, share what you have learned) ~Gichi-Ma'iingan, Obaashiing

On Thursday April 10, 2014 at 11:14 pm, I wrote to Larry Stillday suggesting an opportunity to present one of his teachings. "Larry, I was thinking of your last presentation. You mentioned the health fair for Indian Country to be held at the Sanford Center in June. This might be a good workshop for one of your teachings, no? I mean we're talking about Indians and health. Do you mind if I suggest you be a presenter to the PR guy (Warren Larson) from Sanford I know? Maybe even send him the presentation? It's just a thought."

Larry answered about an hour and a half later Friday morning. "Hey you mean to tell me you were thinking? Isn't that dangerous? It's fine if you want to mention this to that PR person, but I don't know about sending the presentation for the simple reason they might take it and interpret it in a linear way, or try to figure it out that way. I'd be willing to meet with him/her if you want to set it up."

"Yeah, my wife doesn't like me thinking," I wrote back. "I see what you are saying. I will mention it to him. I'll see him on Tuesday at the latest. Shouldn't you be in bed? I don't want you to turn out like me." (I'm a very late night person)

"Thank you for understanding," Larry answered. "That's the reason the old people didn't write down much of the information, because it was turned around and translated in a linear way, which it then lost its major content in the process."

"Hey I made a mistake today," Larry said in response to the late night. "I drank coffee late afternoon, now I'm sitting here with a major Simpson Eyes Syndrome (he was referencing the TV sitcom, the Simpsons). I can't sleep, and I have to get up early to go to Red Lake and do the invocation for the Crime Victim Rights walk. It will start at the Law Enforcement Complex and end at the Boys and Girls Club. There I speak about the violence from the indigenous perspective, there will be other speakers as well. So I really need to do something with this Simpson Eyes Syndrome."

Shortly thereafter I wrote to my friend Warren, the PR guy from Sanford Health. "I just left a message on your work voice mail about considering teacher, healer, cultural, language, spiritual advisor, and elder Larry Stillday on the agenda at the Sanford Health event in June."

The following Monday Warren answered that his team had already contacted Larry in that regard. (I learned later that it was to do an invocation, not a presentation)

On April 30, 2014 Warren sent me a copy of a letter describing the upcoming health research summit he sent out to would-be participants. The summit was to be held Wednesday June 11, 2014 at the Sanford Center in Bemidji, MN.

"Our goal," he wrote, "is to enhance the knowledge and competence of participants by providing an update on the latest strategies regarding the impact of trans-disciplinary research to tribal communities."

The same day I wrote back. "Looks great," I said, "I will naturally promote the heck out of it. My only sadness is that folks will not benefit from what Gichi-Ma'iingan (Larry Stillday) has to offer. Next year your group will know of Larry Stillday, mark my word."

"I am trying to fit in Larry Stillday's presentation on the 10th of June, the pre-summit," Warren answered. "The main Summit is set and can't be changed, but we still have potential for him to present on the 10th. I will let you know if this gets accomplished."

"That sounds wonderful," I responded. I asked Larry if it was okay to drop his name and what his teaching is. He said he would welcome that invitation. "I appreciate what you are doing, thank you."

On May 1, 2014 I sent Larry a copy of Warren's note about fitting Larry in as a presenter at the coming Health Summit of June 10. "Niiji (my friend) FYI." And then I added, (interestingly in hindsight) "Healing Lodge this year?"

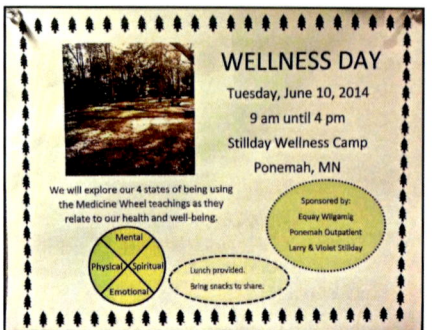

"Hey Niiji, I'm already committed on June 10th," Larry wrote back, "that's the date of our Wellness Day at the lodge. People are starting to prepare for that day."

"Sanford's loss." I answered. "Barb and I and Barry and Linda will be at the Wellness Day at the Lodge. Howa!" (Great)

In reply Larry wrote. "Great! Your presence will make it complete. Are there any areas that you might feel needs to be clarified? Or is there a topic you would be interested to be presented?"

I answered. "Boozhoo Gichi-Ma'iingan. The only thing I can think of is that not many people saw your presentation about "boundaries" at the school, although I will have the story of that presentation available to all probably by the end of next week. I am writing it now, but I want to be careful with the words I use to reflect your teaching in a manner that will be understood.

The "boundaries" thing is so important. It may be what ails the world. Some, like narcissists, think that we all exist for them, and some are so wishy-washy they become what others are. This was a big eye opener for me, although as you have said…I guess I already knew that.

Thank you for asking, but you are the teacher, and all I can say is keep peeling away those layers of the Medicine Wheel. You are doing a very good job. Your words are reaching many. I am going to be selfish and hope that your lodge does not turn into Woodstock and we lose the intimacy of the teaching. Perhaps my concern is unwarranted."

"Hi and thank you," Larry replied. "I should have asked if there was anything I need to review with those who will attend."

"I think a short review is often good," I wrote back. "Remind people where we are. I am one of the few who makes nearly all your presentations. However, like I said earlier, I always write about your teachings/presentations, (with the Chairman's blessing I might add) and then I make sure that all of those who have attended past presentations and who may have missed the latest, get a copy of my stories. I hope that is helpful.

I think I understand my name better now. I saw Vickey (Larry's niece) at the Youth Leadership banquet tonight. I was telling her of my addictions. 'You are addicted to Indians' she said with that wonderfully warm smile of hers. And she is right, hard to quantify, but I know you know what I mean. It is a good thing. I have found my passion."

Two Weeks later on May 16, 2014 (Larry turned 70 on the 14th and would pass on the 20th) my wife Barbara wrote to me. (This would be my last email thread with Larry.)

"I just read in the paper that Darrell (Seki, Sr., newly elected Red Lake Chairman and friend) will be sworn in June 10th. That's the Healing Lodge day also. Do you think Larry will change the Teaching Lodge Day?"

I quickly wrote Larry. "Larry, Will Darrell's swearing-in affect the Healing Lodge schedule?"

"Hey Niiji, nope I won't change the plans, its still a go. Inform everyone. Thanks. Gichi-Ma'iingan."

(Later that afternoon, I was erroneously told that the inauguration would not conflict with the Healing Lodge, and later yet that it would conflict leaving me with the dilemma of having to cover the inaugural as my job of public relations taking me away from the Healing Lodge for half the day. It was a terrible dilemma. Little did I realize the perceived conflict would make no difference.)

"Howa! I learned the Lodge would not be in conflict with Darrell, the inaugural will be held later. There will be a swearing in just for Darrell and Gary (two outright winners) at the Tribal Council meeting. An inaugural for everyone will happen after the run-off election."

I continued. "So is your name Gichi-Ma'iingan and not Chi-Ma'iingan? The language people (Ojibwe revitalization group) have been referring to you as Chi-Ma'iingan.

You asked once a while back if I would have suggestion of what should be covered at next Healing Lodge. I'd like to see more on 'boundaries.' I don't think the Anglo Saxon mind gets that very well. I'd also like to hear more about the value of symbol in ceremony."

"Hey, yes, the Language people are using the southern dialect, Gichi is the northern dialect," Larry explained. "Yes I will be addressing boundaries and the medicine wheel on how it relates to health and wellbeing, which of course includes needing and having boundaries. There is going to be a lot of people there. I got calls from Leech Lake, and some people from and around Bemidji.

All I hope for is that I have enough air in my lungs to speak to all those people. The alternative is to call on you if I run out of air. I'm hoping to have the Language Revitalization project there to do a little Anishinaabe teaching."

"I am excited and afraid that there will be many people at the lodge with the stories written about you and the good response you are getting," I wrote back. "More and more people are interested which is again what we are looking for, no? More and more people are getting interested."

"Afraid of more people? That didn't enter my mind," Larry replied, "but now that you mention it, I guess I will be afraid now too. However, isn't this what it is all about? There are many people out there that are waiting just for something like this."

"Yes, we are the ones we've been waiting for," I wrote.

"True, true, true," Larry replied.

"Be happy to pump air in you when you need it," I volunteered.

"Hey that doesn't sound right," Larry answered.

"Southern dialect maybe?" said I.

And Larry wrote and wrote no more, "That's it, boy, you know some stuff."

I received that last message on Friday, May 16, 2014 at 6:31 pm. In the early morning of May 20th, Larry died peacefully in his sleep, and I never heard from Gichi-Ma'iingan again.

Afterword:
Red Lake: A Unique Sovereignty

All Indian bands have sovereignty roughly on equal par with states, although some tribes in some states are beholden to the state, something known as Public Law 280. The Red Lake Band has a unique sovereignty and only answers, ultimately, to the United States Congress. The reason?

The Red Lake Band resides on aboriginal land and has lived in the area since the Dakota moved from the region in the mid-1700's. In Red Lake's only treaty with the United States in 1863 at Old Crossing, Red Lake ceded 11 million acres of arguably the most fertile land in North America, the Red River Valley, to the United States. Red Lake never ceded the diminished reservation making it unique in Indian Country. Other tribes ceded all lands and then were given it back in the form of reservations. Red Lake is known as a "closed reservation" meaning all land is held in common by the members of the tribe. It is unique, one of only two tribes in the US to hold the status.

During the late 1800's, Red Lake tribal leadership skillfully resisted allotment legislation and held the land intact for the Tribe as a whole. Pike Creek at Red Lake is the site of the historic land agreement of 1889 where seven

determined and foresighted chiefs resisted complying with the Dawes Allotment Act of 1887. (The US quit making treaties with Indians in 1868)

Because of the foresight of Red Lake ancestors who refused to participate in the Dawes Act, Anishinaabe heritage and tradition are preserved. English is a second language to many Red Lake members middle-aged and older including some on the Tribal Council. Ojibwe is being revitalized and spoken at different levels of fluency and is understood by many others. According to Anton Treuer, an author and academic specializing in the Ojibwe language and American Indian studies, states in his book *Ojibwe in Minnesota*, that approximately 60% of the fluent Ojibwe speakers in the US live at Red Lake, most of them at Ponemah. Ponemah is the most Native American census designated location in the United States by Percent.

The diminished reservation is 636,954 acres. Other holdings including the Northwest Angle at 156,900 acres total 825,654 acres, larger than the state of Rhode Island. Red Lake is the largest fresh water lake in the country wholly contained within one state. The lake, Miskwaagamiiwizaaga'iganiing to the Red Lake Ojibwe, is held sacred.

Treaties are Still Legally Binding

"Indians are different from any other group, our status is different, no other group had treaties, and so we are distinguished from other minority groups. We were trading with Europeans long before there was an America, with Spain, France, Netherlands, and England.

The settlers flowing into Red Lake lands were of a new and foreign culture uninterested in the culture of the land and its Indigenous peoples. This was much different from the French who essentially assimilated with First Nation peoples. The French recognized that all Indigenous peoples have something in common, and that is…we owned the North American Continent." ~ Red Lake author and historian Brenda Child, quoting Vine Deloria, famous American Indian author and historian.

Ojibwemowin Revitalization

Loss of language and culture is a main concern of Ojibwe people today. According to Dr. Anton Treuer, professor of Ojibwe at Bemidji State University, in his book entitled *Ojibwe in Minnesota*, estimates that there are fewer than 1000 Ojibwe speakers in the United States with nearly all of them residing in Minnesota, and a majority of them from Red Lake. Treuer estimates that fewer than 100 speakers are left in Michigan, Wisconsin and North Dakota combined.

Although there are thousands of speakers in Canada, language revitalization is becoming a concern there as well. Even within reservations, speakers tend to be concentrated. "Almost all the speakers from Red Lake are from the community of Ponemah", says Treuer. He estimates 675 speakers in Minnesota, 400 of them from Red Lake. "Language and culture go hand in hand", adds Treuer, and points out that there are only a handful of Ojibwe speakers who conduct all traditional funerals in Ojibwe country.

The Red Lake Tribal Council a few years ago voted unanimously to declare Ojibwemowin as the official language of the Red Lake Band of Chippewa Indians, and declared that it is important that the State of Minnesota officially recognize Ojibwe (and Dakota) language as the first languages of the State.

It is important to differentiate this type of effort as an official language from say French as an official language of Canada, or the controversy of Spanish speakers in the southwest. Ojibwe and other Indigenous languages are the original languages of the land and not imported tongues, as are French, Spanish, or English.

Glossary

Can humanity risk losing the ancient knowledge of heaven and earth that may be hidden in the depths of dying languages and cultures? There is no culture without language.

"The loss of languages is tragic precisely because they are not interchangeable, precisely because they represent the distillation of the thoughts and communication of people over their entire history." ~Marianne Mithun

Chippewa - Chippeway - Otchipway - Ojibway - Ojibwa - Ojibwe

The Ojibwe language has different sounds that many may be unfamiliar with. This is because Ojibwemowin does not lend itself to the 26 letter English alphabet. Rules then for pronunciation have been developed using the English alphabet as a base. As one can see demonstrated above, Ojibwe and Chippewa are actually the same word heard and then written differently.

The Double Vowel system is based on the idea that the letters and letter combinations represent Ojibwe sounds, not English sounds even though they are taken from the English alphabet. Each letter or letter combination in the Double Vowel system has only one possible pronunciation, unlike English where the word "read" can be pronounced two different ways with two different meanings.

The system takes its name from its treatment of vowels. There are short vowels and long vowels. The short vowels are formed using one letter, and two letters, or a doubling of the letter, and thus the name "double vowel" forms the long vowels.

At a conference held to discuss the development of a common Ojibwe orthography, Ojibwe language educators agreed that the Double Vowel system was a preferred choice, while recognizing that other systems were also used and preferred in some locations. The Double Vowel system is widely favored among language teachers in the United States and Canada.

There are probably dozens of ways used among the Ojibwe to spell Ojibwemowin, including "Folk Spelling" which is not a system per se, as it varies among first speakers when writing the language. Each writer employing folk spelling would write out the word as how the speaker himself hears the words.

There are First Speakers from Ponemah alone that spell the word frog as muckuckii, muckakee makaki makakii, omakakii and more. It is emphasized that although the "double vowel system" is used in teaching, many first speakers use "folk spelling" and it is NOT wrong, only different. The Nichols/Nyholm Dictionary is the book of reference for the "double vowel system."

Ojibwe is a complex, sophisticated verb based language. It is descriptive which accounts for the many compound words. It is also why the language does not borrow from English when it comes up with new concepts such as "internet."

One example I like to use is the word for coffee, Makade-mashkikiwaaboo, which literaly means "Black Medicine Water." I mentioned this to my friend, a first speakeer, Darrell Seki at one point, and he said; "Does not, means coffee."

One more thing I'd like to share. Perhaps the reason why we see a respect for elders in Indigenous communities is the meaning of the words. The word for "elder" is Gichi-aya'aa, which literally means "Great Being." The word for female elder is Mindimooye, which liteally means; "One who holds things together." And the word for male elder is Akiwenzii, which literally means "Earth Protector." When a culture has words like these to describe "senior citizens," one probably doesn't have to remind their children to respect their elders.

Although the letters used are taken from the English alphabet, they represent Ojibwe sounds, not English sounds. In the examples below, Ojibwe sounds and English approximations of the Ojibwe sounds are given. However, it is always best to consult a native speaker for the best pronunciation. Correct pronunciation is important, mispronouncing a word can completely change its meaning.

The English letters and sounds of f, l, q, r, u, v and x are not part of the Ojibwe alphabet.

The Ojibwe alphabet contains the additional double-letter symbols of aa, ch, ii, oo, sh and zh.

Glossary

The glottal stop (represented by an apostrophe) is a sound made by a release of air from your throat, similar to when someone punches you in the stomach.

Credit for this pronunciation guide goes to Rick Gresczyk (Ojibwe Word List. Eagle Works, Minneapolis, MN) and to John Nichols and Earl Nyholm (A Concise Dictionary of Minnesota Ojibwe).

From

A Concise Dictionary of Minnesota Ojibwe

John D. Nichols and Earl Nyholm

The "Double Vowel System" of Ojibwemowin Spelling

Compiled and Edited by Michael Meuers for Bemidji's Ojibwe Language Project

<u>Ojibwe Alphabetical Order</u>

a, aa, b, c, d, e, g, h, ', i, ii, j, k, m, n, o, oo, p, s, t, w, y, z, (' = glottal stop)

Digraphs = *ch, sh, zh*

<u>Vowels</u>

	<u>Phonetic</u>	<u>Ojibwe Example</u>		<u>English Equivalent</u>
a	[^]	*agim*	'count someone'	about
aa	[a:]	*aagim*	'snowshoe'	father
e	[e:]	*awenen*	'who'	café
i	[I]	*inini*	'man'	pin
ii	[i]	*niin*	'I'	seen
o	[o]~[U]	*anokii*	'works'	obey, book
oo	[o:]~[u:]	*anookii*	'hires'	boat, boot

Glossary

Nasal Vowels

Nasal vowels are indicated by writing the appropriate basic vowel followed by *nh*. Before a *y* or a glottal stop ' the *h* may be omitted in writing. There are no direct English equivalents:

aanh	[a:]	*banajaanh*	'nestling'
enh	[e:]	*nisayenh*	'my older brother'
iinh	[i:]	*awesiinh*	'wild animal'
oonh	[o:]	*giigoonh*	'fish'

Nasalized Vowels

Vowels are nasalized before *ns, nz,* and *nzh*. The *n* is then omitted in pronunciation. A few examples are:

> *gaawiin ingekend**anz**iin* 'I don't know it'
>
> *jiimaan**ens*** 'small boat'
>
> *oskh**anzh**iin* 'someone's fingernail(s)'

Long vowels after a nasal consonant m or n are often nasalized, especially before *s, sh, z,* or *zh*, It is often difficult to decide whether to write these as nasalized vowels or not. For example while we write the word for 'moose ' without indicating the phonetic nasalization, many prefer to write it with an n: *Mooz* or ***moonz*** 'moose'

Consonants and Other Sounds

The non-nasal consonants occur in pairs with one member of the pair a strong consonant and the other member of the pair a weak consonant. The strong consonants do not occur at the beginning of words (unless a vowel is left off), may sound long or double, and are voiceless. The weak consonants can occur at the beginning of words and are often voiced especially in the middle of words.

Glossary

	Phonetic	**Ojibwe Example**	**English Equivalent**
b	[b]~[p]	*bakade* 'is hungry'	**b**ig, s**p**in
ch	[c:]	*miigwech* 'thanks'	sti**ch**
d	[d]~[t]	*debwe* 'tells the truth'	**d**o, s**t**op
g	[g]~[k]	*giin* 'you'	**g**eese, s**k**i
h	[h]	hay 'expression-displeasure'	**h**i
'		*bakite'an* 'hit it!'	
j	[j]	*ajina* 'a little while'	**j**ump
k	[k:]	*amik* 'beaver'	pi**ck**
m	[m]	*miijim* 'food'	**m**an
n	[n]	*naanan* 'five'	**n**ame
	before g,k	*bangii* 'a little bit'	hu**n**ger
p	[p:]	*imbaap* 'I laugh'	ri**p**
s	[s:]	*asin* 'stone, rock'	mi**ss**
sh	[s:]	*animosh* 'dog'	bu**sh**
t	[t:]	*ate* '(something) is there'	pi**t**
w	[w]	*waabang* 'tomorrow'	**w**ay
y	[y]	*inday* 'my dog'	**y**ellow
z	[z]~[s]	*ziibi* 'river'	**z**ebra
zh	[z]~[s]	*biizh* 'bring someone!'	mea**s**ure

Consonant Clusters

sk	[sk]	*miskozi* 'is red'	
shp	[sp]	*ishpiming* 'up above, in heaven	
sht	[st]	*nishtigwaan* 'my head'	
shk	[sk]	*ishkode* 'fire'	

Glossary

mb	[mb]	*wii**mb**aa* 'is hollow'
nd	[nd]	*aa**nd**i* 'where'
nj	[nj]	*nini**nj*' 'my hand'
ng	[ng]	*ba**ng**ii* 'a little bit'

A single consonant (except *w*, *h*, and *y*) or a consonant cluster may be followed by *w* before a vowel. A few examples are ***b**waan* 'Dakota', *op**waagan* 'pipe', ***gwii**wizens* 'boy', **ami**kwag** 'beavers', *nis**wi* 'three', *bagida'**waa*'sets a net', *mis**kwi* 'blood', and *bing**wi* 'sand, ashes'.

Ojibwemowin Words from the Book and for Fun

"It's every bit a treasure as any ancient artifact, how much more vital is it to have a living breathing language that tells us how life evolved here on this very continent." ~Louise Erdrich, Ojibwe Writer, Turtle Mountain Band of Chippewa Indians.

"If we lose the language, we are no more, we may become something else, but we will not be Anishinaabe." ~Walt Bressette, Red Cliff Ojibwe

The Four Aspects of Development

Inendamowin = Emotional

Manidoowendamowin = Spiritual

Inamanji'owin = Physical

Naanaagadawendamowin = Mental

Colors/Four races

Ozaawaa = Yellow

Miskwaa = Red

Glossary

Makadewaa = Black

Waabishkaa = White

The Cycle of Life (Larry's spellings in parenthesis then double vowel = A. Treuer)

Baby = (abinooji) = abinoojiinh

Youth = (Oshkiniigii) = oshki-aya'aa

Adult = (Gichi-aya'aa) = gichi-aya'aa

Elder = (Gete-ayaa) = gete-aya'aa

(Some speakers' use gichi-aya'aa for elder and gete-aya'aa for "old timer." ~A. Treuer)

First Family

Grandfather Sun = Gimishoomisinaan Giizis

Grandmother Moon = Gookomisinaan Dibiki-giizis

Father Sky = (Ishpiming) = Noosinaan Giizhig

Mother Earth = (Gidakiminoon) = Gimaamaanaan Aki

Center or Self = (Naawayi'ii) = Naawayi'ii

(All terms of relation have to be possessed so these are given in the inclusive "us" form = our mother earth, our grandfather sun, etc. ~A. Treuer)

Directions/Four Winds

Waabanong = East

Zhaawanong = South

Ningaabiiwanong = West

Giiwedinong = North

Glossary

Places

Bemijigamaag = Lake that traverses another body of water (Bemidji)

Gichi-Ziibi = Mississippi River (Big River)

Gidishkoniganina = Red Lake Nation

Maadaabiimong = Redby

Ogaakaaning = Red Lake

Gaa-asiniisikaag = Little Rock

Obaashiing = Ponemah

Miskwaagamiiwizaaga'iganiing = The Red Lake Reservation and/or Lake

Phrases

Oshkaabewis = "the messenger" or "ceremonial attendant"

Bebaanaajimod = he who tells the news

Mino-bimaadiziwin = the good life

Nitaawigi'iwewin maajiigin = the growth/development of being (the four aspects)

Weweni = carefully

Gigaagiigidotamaagoom, maada'ooyok gaa-miinigooyeg. = You are speakers for us now, share what you have learned

Bawaajigewin = Vision (or Dream) Quest

Nitaawigi'iwewin = Child Raising

Ganawenindizowinan = Self Care Teachings

Gakeyaa Ashinaajimoyeg = How you all say things/put things

Boozhoo niijanishinaabedog, giwii-piindigemin madoodooswaning noongom = Hello my fellow Indians, we will enter the sweat lodge today. Thank you all for coming.

Glossary

Miigwech wii-nanda-gikinoo'aamagoziyeg = Thank you all for striving to learn.

Gigii-miinigoomin gakina gegoo ji-mino-bimaadiziyang mewinzha. = Long ago we were given everything to live a good life

Red Lake Reservation on the Medicine Wheel

Miskwaagamiiwizaaga'iganiing = (Lake of Red liquid) Red Lake, (Lake and Reservation)

Maadaabiimong = (Landing Place) Redby in the East

Ogaakaaning = (Place of walleye) Red Lake Village to the south

Gaa-asiniisikaag = (place of many stones?) Little Rock to the west

Obaashiing = (Windy Point) Ponemah in the north

Red Lake's Seven Clans

Awaazisii = Bullhead

Makwa = Black Bear

Migizi = Bald Eagle

Mikinaak = Snapping Turtle

Nigig = Otter

Ogiishkimanisii = Kingfisher

Waabizheshi = Pine Marten

Sacred Medicines

Tobacco = Asemaa

Sage = Mashkode-wiingashk

Cedar = Giizhik

Sweet grass = Wiingashk

Glossary

Medicine = Mashkiki (add wan for plural)

Kinnickinnic = is an Ojibwe word which literally means "what is mixed," referring to the mixing of indigenous plants and tobaccos as opposed to what mostly is used asemaa or tobacco.

Seasons

Ziigwan = Spring

Niibin = Summer

Dagwaagin = Autumn

Biboon = Winter

Teachings

Gikinoo'amaagewwinnaan = Teachings

Niizhwaaso Mishoomis Gikinoo'amaagewwinnaan = The Teachings of the Seven Grandfathers ~Larry

Niizhwaaswi Gimishoomisinaanig Ogikinoo'amaadiwiniwaan = The Teachings of Our Seven Grandfathers ~A. Treuer (Double Vowel)

Seven Teachings, Larry

- Nbwaakaawin (Wisdom)
- Zaagi'idiwin (Love)
- Minwaadendamowin (Respect)
- Aakwade'ewin (Bravery or Courage)
- Gwekwaadizwin (Honesty)
- Dabbadendiziwin (Humility)
- Debwewin (Truth)

Seven Teachings, A. Treuer (Double Vowel)

- Nibwaakaawin (Wisdom)
- Zaagi'idiwin (Love)
- Manaajitwaawin (Respect)
- Zoongide'ewin (Bravery or Courage)
- Gwayakowaadiziwin (Honesty)
- Dabasenindizowin (Humility)
- Debwewin (Truth)

Seven Teachings Animals

Amik = Beaver

Ma'iingan = Wolf

Makwa = Black Bear

Mashkode Bizhiki = Bison/Buffalo

Migizi = Bald Eagle

Mikinaak = Snapping Turtle

Misaabe = Giant or Big Foot

Other Ojibwe Words, Anishaa (Just for Fun)

Animals = Awesiyag

Ajijaak = Crane

Animosh = Dog

Gaazhagens = Cat

Omakakii = Frog

Waawaashkeshi = Deer

Glossary

Chitchat

Please = Daga or Indaga)

Miigwech = Thank you

Miigwech gayegiin = you're welcome!

Mino-giizhigad = it's a good or nice day

Howa = "awesome" or "cool"

Aho is an expression of acknowledgment like "all right"

Common Introduction

Aaniin ezhinikaazoyan? = What is your name?

_____ indizhinikaaz = my name is _____.

Aandi wenjibaayan? = Where are you from?

_____ indoonjibaa = I am from_____.

Awenen gidoodem? = Who is your clan?

_____Indoodem = my clan is _____

Foods: (plural is in parentheses)
Apple = Mishiimin (ag)

Baking = Gibozigewin

Beans = Mashkodesimin (ag)

Bread = Bakwezhigan (ag)

Cake = Wiishkoobi-bakwezhigan

Candy = Ziinzibaakwad

Carrot = Okaadaak (oon)

Cheese = Doodooshaaboowimiijim

Cleaning = biinichigewin

Glossary

Chocolate = Ozaawi-ziinzibaakwad

Chocolate = Ozaawi-wiishkoobanjigan
Foods – Wiisiniwinan

Flour = Bakwezhigan (ag)

Grain = Miinikaanens (an)

Herbs = Degonigaadeg (in)

Lettuce = Aniibiish (an)

Maple Syrup = Zhiiwaagamizigan

Meat = Wiiyaas (an)
Milk = Doodooshaaboo

Pizza = Niiyo-biitoosijigan

Potato = Opin

Roots = Jiibikoon
Spice = Anooj dino gaa-wiisagang

Tea = Aniibiish (an)
Tea, black = Makade-aniibiish
Tea, green = Ozhaawashko-aniibiish

Waffle = Waashkoobi-gakakaag
White Rice = Waabi-manoomin
Wild Rice = Manoomin

Months

Gichi-manidoo-giizis or manidoo-giizis = January

Namebini-giizis = February

Onaabani-giizis = March

Iskigamizige-giizis = April

Waabigwanii-giizis = May

Ode'imini-giizis = June

Glossary

Aabita-niibino-giizis = July

Manoomininike-giizis = August

Waatebagaa-giizis = September

Binaakwii-giizis = October

Gashkadino-giizis = November

Manidoo-giizisoons = December

Days = Giizhigoon

Nights = Dibiikadoon

Numbers

Bezhig = one

Niizh = two

Niswi = three

Niiwin = four

Naanan = five

Ningodwaaswi = six

Niizhwaaso = seven

Ishwaaso = eight

Zhaangaso = nine

Midaaswi = ten

Phrases

Gidinawemidimin = We are all related.

Mii iw waa-ikidoyaan. = That's all I have to say.

Waasa Inaabidaa = We Look In All Directions.

Mino-bimaadizin — Moozhag Baapin — Apane Zhawenjigen = Live

Glossary

Well – Laugh Often – Love Much.

Relationships

Wiijiw- or (niwiiw, my wife) is a partner, wife, friend, so in this case it means those people who "walk with you."

Niiji or Niij = male friend of male

Nimise = older brother or male's female friend or older sister

Nishime = little brother/male's younger woman friend/sister

Ninjjiwaam = good friend (forever)

Gichi-aya'aa = great being (elder)

Mindimooye = one who holds things together = female elder (family matriarch)

Akiwenzii = earth caretaker = male elder

Gichi-mookomaan (an) = a white person an American (literally Big Knife)

Culture and Language

On Ojibwe Dialects

Larry's Spirit (or Indian) name is Gichi-Ma'iingan meaning Great or Big Wolf. He signed his Spirit name in several different ways, Ma'iingan, or more often Chi-Ma'iingan, and Gichi-Ma'iingan, sometimes using the hyphen and sometimes not. Many also referred to him by one of these names. His name spelled using the accepted double vowel system, is Gichi-Ma'iingan the northern Ojibwe and Ponemah dialect, Chi- would be southern dialect. Gichi-Ma'iingan therefore is the name I use outside of quotes.

From epilogue: "So is your name Gichi-Ma'iingan and not Chi-Ma'iingan? The language people (Ojibwe revitalization group) have been referring to you as Chi-Ma'iingan."

"Hey, yes, the Language people are using the southern dialect, Gichi is the northern dialect."

Glossary

Acknowledgments

For Unwavering Moral Support

Much thanks to my wife Barbara Meuers, Larry's widow Violet Stillday, and my good friends Barry & Linda Babcock, and Eugene "Bugger" McArthur.

For Encouragement and Feedback

Thanks to my daughters Kimberly Irene and Erin Marie, sister-in-law Cynthia Meuers, cousin Frank Meuers, and friends Rachelle Houle, Rozanna Landavazo, Bobbie Harrington, Lorraine Cecil, David Harrington, Donna Hoffer, Jeanne Edevold Larson, and Frank Moe.

For Treating Me Like Kinfolk

Gichi-Miigwech to the family of Larry Stillday; Rose Cloud, Wesley Cloud, Vickey Fineday, Randy & Marna Stillday, Larry Stillday, Jr., Leigh Stillday, James Cloud, and Elliott Cloud

For Ojibwemowin Translations and Spellings

Miigwech to Anton Treuer and Eugene Stillday

For Sharing Photos/Videos

Grateful appreciation to Barbara Meuers, Amy DeGeneres Tanner, Jen Kruse, John Parsons, Scott Knudson, and Julia Huffman.

For Helping Me to Grasp the Complexities of Writing and Publishing:

Much obliged to Laura Drew, Will Weaver, Leo Soukup, and John Eggers.

For Agreeing to be My Editor, Publisher and Friend

A very special miigwech/thank you to Daniel Rice of Riverfeet Press. I'm grateful that he not only agreed to take on this assignment, but he accomplished the even greater challenge of "getting me" and the book I envisioned. He walked me through this process with patience, professionalism, encouragement, and imagination.

Meuers lives with his wife, three cats and a dog on a four-acre peninsula overlooking the Mississippi River just after it leaves Lake Bemidji. They have two adult daughters and two grandchildren. He grew up in the Twin Cities moving to Minnesota's Great North Woods in his early 30's. He first lived near Northome, MN where he built a house having more time than money. A few years later he had the house moved 55 miles to it's current location on the Mississippi River near Bemidji, MN.

He worked for a local public television affiliate before taking a job with the Red Lake Band of Chippewa Indians. He has worked as a public relations person with the Band for 22 years taking photos and writing stories about the Red Lake Band.

He has worked in a variety of ways to help bridge Indian and Non-Indian culture of north central Minnesota, by encouraging learning, the celebration of diversity, and to open a dialog that would begin this conversation.

He spearheaded Bemidji's Ojibwe Language Project. Nearly 200 businesses and organizations within a hundred miles of Bemidji post a variety of common signage in both English and Ojibwe through his efforts.

Meuers received a Spirit (Indian) name in a ceremony conducted by the book's subject, Larry Stillday, in the summer of 2013. Biidaanakwad Izhinikaazo. (Gathering Cloud is His Name).

Meuers operates a blog, titled: Indian Country, Through the Eyes of an Irishman. You can find it here: http://omakakii.blogspot.com/

For more information on this title, or other books from
Riverfeet Press, please visit our webpage:

www.riverfeetpress.com

Bemidji, MN
Livingston, MT
Printed in the U.S.A.